Lewis Carroll in Wonderland and at Home

The Story of his Life

MAVEN BOOKS

Lewis Carroll in Wonderland and at Home

The Story of His Life

Belle Moses

MAVEN BOOKS

Chennai   Trichy   Tirunelveli   New Delhi

MAVEN BOOKS

An Imprint of **MJP Publishers**

ISBN 978-93-87867-36-9   **Maven Books**

All rights reserved   No. 44, Nallathambi Street,
Printed and bound in India   Triplicane, Chennai 600 005

MJP 623   © Publishers, 2019

Publisher : C. Janarthanan

To

E. M. M. and M. J. M.

Publisher's Note

The legacy of a country is in its varied cultural heritage, historical literature, developments in the field of economy and science. The top nations in the world are competing in the field of science, economy and literature. This vast legacy has to be conserved and documented so that it can be bestowed to the future generation. The knowledge of this legacy is slowly getting perished in the present generation due to lack of documentation.

Keeping this in mind, the concern with retrospective acquiring of rare books has been accented recently by the burgeoning reprint industry. Maven Books is gratified to retrieve the rare collections with a view to bring back those books that were landmarks in their time.

In this effort, a series of rare books would be republished under the banner, "Maven Books". The books in the reprint series have been carefully selected for their contemporary usefulness as well as their historical importance within the intellectual. We reconstruct the book with slight enhancements made for better presentation, without affecting the contents of the original edition.

Most of the works selected for republishing covers a huge range of subjects, from history to anthropology. We believe this reprint edition will be a service to the numerous researchers and practitioners active in this fascinating field. We allow readers to experience the wonder of peering into a scholarly work of the highest order and seminal significance.

Maven Books

LEWIS CARROLL

Introduction

Lewis Carroll discovered a new country, simply by rowing up and down the river, and telling a story to the accompaniment of dipping oars and rippling waters, as the boat glided through. It is not everyone who can discover a country, people it with marvelous, fanciful shapes, and give it a place in our mental geography. But Lewis Carroll was not "everyone"—in fact he was like no one else to the many who called him friend. He had the magic power of creating something out of nothing, and gave to the eager children who had tired of "Aunt Louisa's Picture Books," and "Garlands of Poetry," something to think about, to guess about, and to talk about.

If he had written nothing else but "Alice in Wonderland," that one book would have been quite enough to make him famous, but his pen was never idle, and the world of children has much for which to thank him. How much, and for what, the following pages will strive to tell, and if they succeed in conveying to their readers half the charm that lay in the life of this man, who did so much for others, they will not have been written in vain.

In telling the story of his life I am indebted to many, for courtesy and assistance. I wish specially to thank my brother, Montrose J. Moses. Columbia Library, Astor Library, St. Agnes Branch of the Public Library, and Miss Brown, of the Traveling Library, have all been exceedingly kind and helpful. To Messrs. E. P. Dutton and Company I extend my thanks for permission to quote from Miss Isa Bowman's interesting reminiscences, and to the American and English editors of *The Strand* I am also indebted for a similar courtesy.

Belle Moses.

New York, *October, 1910.*

Contents

Chapter I

There was Once a Little Boy

There was once a little boy whose name was *not* Lewis Carroll. He was christened Charles Lutwidge Dodgson, in the parish church of Daresbury, England, where he was born, on January 27, 1832. A little out-of-the-way village was Daresbury, a name derived from a word meaning oak, and Daresbury was certainly famous for its beautiful oaks.

The christening of Baby Charles must have been a very happy occasion. To begin with, the tiny boy was the first child of what proved to be a "numerous family," and the officiating clergyman was the proud papa. The name of Charles had been bestowed upon the eldest son for generations of Dodgsons, who had carried it honorably through the line, handing it down untarnished to this latest Charles, in the parish church at Daresbury.

The Dodgsons could doubtless trace their descent much further back than a great-great-grandfather, being a race of gentlemen and scholars, but the Rev. Christopher Dodgson, who lived quite a century before Baby Charles saw the light, is the earliest ancestor we hear of, and he held a living in Yorkshire. In those days, a clergyman was dependent upon some noble patron for his living, a living meaning the parish of which he had charge and the salary he received for his work, and so when the Rev. Christopher's eldest son Charles also took holy orders, he had for *his* patron the Duke of Northumberland, who gave him the living of Elsden in Northumberland, a cold, bleak, barren country. The Rev. Charles took what fell to his lot with much philosophy and a saving sense of humor.

He suffered terribly from the cold despite the fact that he snuggled down between two feather beds in the big parlor, which was no doubt the best room in a most uncomfortable house. It was all he could do to keep from freezing, for the doors were rarely closed against the winds that howled around them. The good clergyman was firmly convinced that the end of the world would come by frost instead of fire. Even when safely in bed, he never felt *quite* comfortable unless his head was wrapped in three nightcaps, while he twisted a pair of stockings, like a cravat, around his suffering throat. He generally wore two shirts at a time, as washing was cheap, and rarely took off his coat and his boots.

This uncomplaining, jovial clergyman finally received his reward. King George III bestowed upon him the See of Elphin, which means that he was made bishop, and had no more hardships to bear. This gentleman, who was the great-grandfather of our Charles, had four children; Elizabeth Anne, the only daughter, married a certain Charles Lutwidge of Holmrook in Cumberland. There were two sons who died quite young, and Charles, the eldest, entered the army and rose to the rank of captain in the 4th Dragoon Guards. He lost his life in the performance of a perilous duty, leaving behind him two sons; Charles, the elder, turned back into the ways of his ancestors and became a clergyman, and Hassard, who studied law, had a brilliant career.

This last Charles, in 1830, married his cousin, Frances Jane Lutwidge, and in 1832 we find him baptizing another little Charles, in the parish church at Daresbury, his eldest son, and consequently his pride and hope.

The living at Daresbury was the beginning of a long life of service to the Church. The father of our Charles rose to be one of the foremost clergymen of his time, a man of wide learning, of deep piety, and of great charity, beloved by rich and poor. Though of somewhat sober nature, in moments of recreation he could throw off his cares like a boy, delighting his friends by his wit and humor, and the rare gift of telling anecdotes, a gift his son inherited in full measure, long before he took the name of "Lewis Carroll," some twenty years after he was received into the fold of the parish church at Daresbury.

Little Charles headed the list of eleven young Dodgsons, and the mother of this infant brigade was a woman in a thousand. We all know what mothers are; then we can imagine this one, so kind and gentle that never a harsh word was known to pass her lips, and may be able to trace her quiet, helpful influence on the character of our Boy, just as we see her delicate features reproduced in many of his later pictures.

A boy must be a poor specimen, indeed, if such a father and mother could not bring out the best in him. Saddled as he was, with the responsibility of being the oldest of eleven, and consequently an example held up to younger brothers and sisters, Charles was grave and serious beyond his years. Only an eldest child can appreciate what a responsibility this really is. You mustn't do "so and so" for fear one of the younger ones might do likewise! If his parents had not been very remarkable people, this same Charles might have developed into a virtuous little prig. "Good Brother Charles who never does wrong" might have grown into a terrible bugbear to the other small Dodgsons, had he not been brimful of fun and humor himself. As it was he soon became their leader in all their games and plays, and the quiet parsonage on the glebe farm, full a mile and a half from even the small traffic of the village, rang at least with the echoes of laughter and chatter from these youngsters with strong healthy lungs.

We cannot be quite sure whether they were good children or bad children, for time somehow throws a halo around childhood, but let us hope they were "jes' middlin'." We cannot bear to think of all those prim little saints, with ramrods down their backs, sitting sedately of a Sunday in the family pew—perhaps it took two family pews to hold them—with folded hands and pious expressions. We can't believe these Dodgsons were so silly; they were reverent little souls doubtless, and probably were not bad in church, but oh! let us hope they got into mischief sometimes. There was plenty of room for it in the big farm parsonage.

> "An island farm 'mid seas of corn,
> Swayed by the wand'ring breath of morn.
> The happy spot where I was born,"

wrote Lewis Carroll many years after, when "Alice in Wonderland" had made him famous.

Glebe farms were very common in England; they consisted of large tracts of land surrounding the parsonage, which the pastor was at liberty to cultivate for his own use, or to eke out his often scanty income, and as the parsonage at Daresbury was comparatively small, and the glebe or farm lands fairly large, we can be sure these boys and girls loved to be out of doors, and little Charlie at a very early age began to number some queer companions among his intimate friends. His small hands burrowing in the soft, damp earth, brought up squirming, wriggling things—earthworms, snails, and the like. He made pets of them, studying their habits in his "small boy" way, and having long, serious talks with them, lying on the ground beside them as they crawled around him. An ant-hill was to him a tiny town, and many a long hour the child must have spent busying himself in their small affairs, settling imaginary disputes, helping the workers, supplying provisions in the way of crumbs, and thus early beginning to understand the ways of the woodland things about which he loved to write in after years. He had, for boon companions, certain toads, with whom he held animated conversations, and it is said that he really taught earthworms the art of warfare by supplying them with small pieces of pipe with which to fight.

He did not, like Hiawatha in the legend, "Learn of ev'ry bird its language," but he invented a language of his own, in which no doubt he discoursed wisely to the toads and snails who had time to listen; he learned to speak this language quite fluently, so that in later years when eager children clustered about him, and with wide eyes and peals of laughter listened to his nonsense verses, full of the queerest words they ever heard, they could still understand from the very tones of his voice exactly what he meant. Indeed, when little Charles Lutwidge Dodgson grew up to be Lewis Carroll, he worked this funny language of his by equally funny rules, so that, as he said, "a perfectly balanced mind could understand it."

Of course, there were other companions for the Dodgson children—cats and dogs, and horses and cows, and in the village of Warrington, seven miles away, there were children to be found of their own size and age, but Daresbury itself was very lonely. A canal ran through the far end of the parish, and here bargemen used to ply to and fro, carrying produce and fodder to the near-by towns. Mr. Dodgson took a keen interest in these men who seemed to have no settled place of worship.

In a quiet, persuasive way he suggested to Sir Francis Egerton, a large landholder of the country, that it would be nice to turn one of the barges into a chapel, describing how it could be done for a hundred pounds, well knowing, clever man, that he was talking to a most interested listener; for a few weeks later he received a letter from Sir Francis telling him that the chapel was ready. In this odd little church, the first of its kind, Mr. Dodgson preached every Sunday evening.

But at Daresbury itself life was very monotonous; even the passing of a cart was a great event, and going away was a great adventure. There was one never-to-be-forgotten occasion when the family went off on a holiday jaunt to Beaumaris. Railroads were then very rare things, so they made the journey in three days by coach, allowing also three days for the return trip.

It was great fun traveling in one of those old-time coaches with all the luggage strapped behind, and all the bright young faces atop, and four fast-trotting horses dashing over the ground, and a nice long holiday with fine summer weather to look forward to. But in winter, in those days, traveling was a serious matter; only a favored few could squeeze into the body of the coach; the others still sat atop, muffled to the chin, yet numb with the cold, as the horses went faster and faster, and the wind whistled by, and one's breath froze on the way. Let us hope the little Dodgsons went in the summer time.

Daresbury must have been a beautiful place, with its pleasant walks, its fine meadows, its deep secluded woods, and best of all, those wonderful oak trees which the boy loved to climb, and under whose shade he would lie by the hour, filling his head with all those quaint fancies which he has since given to the world. He was a clever little fellow, eager to learn, and from the first his father superintended his education, being himself a scholar of very high order. He had the English idea of sending his eldest son along the path he himself had trod; first to a public school, then to Oxford, and finally into the Church, if the boy had any leaning that way.

Education in those days began early, and not by way of the kindergarten; the small boy had scarcely lost his baby lisp before he was put to the study of Latin and Greek, and Charles, besides, developed a passion for mathematics. It is told that when a very small boy he showed his father a book of logarithms, asking him to explain it, but Mr. Dodgson mildly though firmly refused.

"You are too young to understand such a difficult subject," he replied; "a few years later you will enjoy the study—wait a while."

"*But*," persisted the boy, his mind firmly bent on obtaining information, "please explain." Whether the father complied with his request is not recorded, but we rather believe that explanations were set aside for the time. Certain it is, they were demanded again and again, for the boy soon developed a wonderful head for figures and signs, a knowledge which grew with the years, as we shall see later.

When he was still quite a little boy, his mother and father went to Hull to visit Mrs. Dodgson's father who had been ill. The children, some five or six in number—the entire eleven had not yet arrived—were left in the care of an accommodating aunt, but Charles, being the eldest, received a letter from his mother in which he took much pride, his one idea being to keep it out of the clutches of his little sisters, whose hands were always ready for mischief. He wrote upon the back of the note, forbidding them to touch his property, explaining cunningly that it was covered with slimy pitch, a most uncomfortable warning, but it was "the ounce of prevention," for the letter has been handed down to us, and a sweet, cheery letter it was, so full of mother-love and care, and tender pride in the little brood at home. No wonder he prized it!

This is probably the first letter he ever received, and it takes very little imagination to picture the important air with which he carried it about, and the care with which he hoarded it through all the years.

There is a dear little picture of our Boy taken when he was eight years old. Photography was not yet in use, so this black print of him is the copy of a silhouette which was the way people had their "pictures taken" in those days. It was always a profile picture, and little Charles's finely shaped head, with its slightly bulging forehead and delicate features, stands sharply outlined. We have also a silhouette of Mrs. Dodgson, and the resemblance between the two is very marked.

When the boy was eleven, a great change came into his life. Sir Robert Peel, the famous statesman, presented to his father the Crown living of Croft, a Yorkshire village about three miles from Darlington. A Crown living is always an exceptionally good one, as it is usually given by royal favor, and accompanied by a comfortable salary. Mr. Dodgson was sorry to leave his old parishioners and the little parsonage where he had seen so much quiet happiness, but he was glad at the same time, to get away from the dullness and monotony of Daresbury. With a growing family of children it was absolutely necessary to come more into contact with people, and Croft was a typical, delightful English town, famous even to-day for its baths and medicinal waters. Before Mr. Dodgson's time it was an important posting-station for the coaches running between London and Edinburgh, and boasted of a fine hotel near the rectory, used later by gentlemen in the hunting season.

Mr. Dodgson's parish consisted not only of Croft proper, but included the neighboring hamlets of Halnaby, Dalton and Stapleton, so he was a pretty busy man going from one to the other, and the little Dodgsons were busy, too, making new friends and settling down into their new and commodious quarters.

The village of Croft is on the river Tees, in fact it stands on the dividing line between Yorkshire and Durham. A bridge divides the two counties, and midway on it is a stone which marks the boundary line. It was an old custom for certain landholders to stand on this bridge at the coming of each new Bishop of Durham, and to present him with an old sword, with an appropriate address of welcome. This sword the Bishop returned immediately.

The Tees often overflowed its banks—indeed, floods were not infrequent in these smiling English landscape countries, kept so fertile and green by the tiny streams which intersect them. Two or three heavy rainfalls will swell the waters, sending them rushing over the country with enormous force. Jean Ingelow in her poem "High Tide on the Coast of Lincolnshire" paints a vivid picture of the havoc such a flood may make in a peaceful land:

"Where the river, winding down,
Onward floweth to the town."

But the quaint old church at Croft has doubtless weathered more than one overflow from the restless river Tees.

The rectory, a large brick house, with a sloping tile roof and tall chimneys, stood well back in a very beautiful garden, filled with all sorts of rare plants, intersected by winding gravel paths. As in all English homes, the kitchen garden was a most attractive spot; its high walls were covered with luxuriant fruit trees, and everybody knows that English "wall fruit" is the most delicious kind. The trees are planted very close to the wall, and the spreading boughs, when they are heavy with the ripening fruit, are not bent with the weight of it, but are thoroughly propped and supported by these walls of solid brick, so the undisturbed fruit comes to a perfect maturity without any of the accidents which occur in the ordinary orchard. The garden itself was bright with kitchen greens, filled with everything needed for household use.

With so much space the little Dodgsons had room to grow and "multiply" to the full eleven, and fine times they had with plays and games, usually invented by their clever brother. One of the principal diversions was a toy railroad with "stations" built at various sections of the garden, usually very pretty and rustic looking, planned and built by Charles himself. He also made a rude train out of a wheelbarrow, a barrel, and a small truck, and was able to convey his passengers comfortably from station to station, exacting fare at each trip.

He was something of a conjurer, too, and in wig and gown, could amaze his audience for hours with his inexhaustible supply of tricks. He also made some quaint-looking marionettes, and a theater for them to act in, even writing the plays, which were masterpieces in their way. Once he traced a maze upon the snow-covered lawn of the rectory.

Mazes were often found in the real old-time gardens of England; they consisted of intersecting paths bordered by clipped shrubbery and generally arranged in geometrical designs, very puzzling to the unwary person who got lost in them, unable to discover a way out, until by some happy accident the right path was found. "Threading the Maze" was a fashionable pastime in the days of the Tudors; the maze at Hampton Court being one of the most remarkable of that period.

Charles's early knowledge of mathematics made his work on the snow-covered lawn all the more remarkable, for the love of that particular branch of learning certainly grew with his growth.

Meanwhile, it was a very serious, earnest little boy, who looked down the long line of Dodgsons, saying with a choke in his voice: "I must leave you and this lovely rectory, and this fair, smiling countryside, and go to school."

He was shy, and the thought struck terror; but everybody who is anybody in England goes to some fine public school before becoming an Oxford or a Cambridge student, and for that reason Charles Lutwidge Dodgson buried his regrets beneath a smiling face, bade farewell to his household, and at the mature age of twelve, armed with enough Greek and Latin to have made a dictionary, with a knowledge of mathematics that a college "don" might well have envied, set forth to this alluring world of books and learning.

Chapter II

School Days at Richmond and Rugby

With the removal to Croft, Mr. Dodgson was brought more and more into prominence; he was appointed examining chaplain to the Bishop of Ripon, and finally he was made Archdeacon of Richmond and one of the Canons of Ripon Cathedral.

The Grammar School at Richmond was well known in that section of England. It was under the rule of a certain Mr. Tate, whose father, Dr. Tate, had made the school famous some years before, and it was there that our Boy had his first taste of school life.

Holidays in those days were not arranged as they are now, for one of the first letters of Charles, sent home from Richmond, was dated August 5th; so it is probable that the term began in midsummer. This special letter was written to his two eldest sisters and gives an excellent picture of those first days, when as a "new boy" he suffered at the hands of his schoolmates. As advanced as he was in Latin and Greek and mathematics, this letter, for a twelve-year-old boy, does not show any remarkable progress in English. The spelling was precise and correct, but the punctuation was peculiar, to say the least.

Still his description of the school life, when one overcame the presence of commas and the absence of periods, presented a vivid picture to the mind. He tells of the funny tricks the boys played upon him because he was a "new boy." One was called "King of the Cobblers." He was told to sit on the ground while the boys gathered around him and to say "Go to work"; immediately they all fell upon him, and kicked and knocked him about pretty roughly. Another trick was "The Red Lion," and was played in the churchyard; they made a mark on a tombstone and one of the boys ran toward it with his finger pointed and eyes shut, trying to see how near he could get to the mark. When *his* turn came, and he walked toward the tombstone, some boy who stood ready beside it, had his mouth open to bite the outstretched finger on its way to the mark. He closes his letter by stating three uncomfortable things connected with his arrival—the loss of his toothbrush and his failure to clean his teeth for several days in consequence; his inability to find his blotting-paper, and his lack of a shoe-horn.

The games the Richmond boys played—football, wrestling, leapfrog and fighting—he slurred over contemptuously, they held no attraction for him.

A schoolboy or girl of the present day can have no idea of the discomforts of school life in Charles Dodgson's time, and the boy whose gentle manners were the result of sweet home influence and association with girls, found the rough ways of the English schoolboy a constant trial. Strong and active as he was, he was always up in arms for those weaker and smaller than himself. Bullying enraged him, and distasteful as it was, he soon learned the art of using his fists for the protection of himself and others. These were the school-days of *Nicholas Nickleby, David Copper-field*, and *Little Paul Dombey*. Of course, all schoolmasters were not like *Squeers* or *Creakle*, nor all schoolmasters' wives like *Mrs. Squeers*, nor indeed all schools like Dotheboys' Hall or Salem Hall, or *Dr. Blimber's* cramming establishment, but many of the inconveniences were certainly prominent in the best schools.

Flogging was considered the surest road to knowledge; kind, honest, liberal-minded teachers kept a birch-rod and a ferrule within gripping distance, and the average schoolboy thus treated like a little beast, could be pardoned for behaving like one. In spring or summer the big, bare, comfortless schoolhouses were all very well, but when the days grew chill, the small boy shivered on his hard bench in his draughty corner, and in winter time the scarcity of fires was trying to ordinary flesh and blood. The poor unfortunate who rose at six, and had to fetch and carry his own water from an outdoor pump, or if he had taken the precaution to draw it the night before, had found it frozen in his pitcher, was not to be blamed if washing was merely a figure of speech.

Mr. and Mrs. Tate were most considerate to their boys, and Richmond was a model school of its class. Charles loved his "kind old schoolmaster" as he called him, and he was not alone in this feeling, for Mr. Tate's influence over the boys was maintained through the affection and respect they had for him. Of course he let them "fight it out" among themselves according to the boy-nature; but the earnest little fellow with the grave face and the eager, questioning eyes, attracted him greatly, and he began to study him in his keen, kind way, finding much to admire and praise in the letters which he wrote to his father, and predicting for him a bright career. Admitting that he had found young Dodgson superior to other boys, he wisely suggested that he should never know this fact, but should learn to love excellence for its own sake, and not for the sake of excelling.

Charles made quite a name for himself during those first school days. Mathematics still fascinated him and Latin grew to be second nature; he stood finely in both, and while at Richmond he developed another taste, the love of composition, often contributing to the school magazine. The special story recorded was called "The Unknown One," but doubtless many a rhyme and jingle which could be traced to him found its way into this same little magazine, not forgetting odd sketches which he began to do at a very early age. They were all rough, for the most part grotesque, but full of simple fun and humor, for the quiet studious schoolboy loved a joke.

Charles stayed at the Richmond school for three years; then he took the next step in an English boy's life, he entered Rugby, one of the great public schools.

In America, a public school is a school for the people, where free instruction is given to all alike; but the English public school is another thing. It is a school for gentlemen's sons, where tuition fees are far from small, and "extras" mount up on the yearly bills.

Rugby had become a very celebrated school when the great Dr. Arnold was Head-Master. Up to that time it was neither so well known nor so popular as Eton, but Dr. Arnold had governed it so vigorously that his hand was felt long after his untimely death, which occurred just four years before Charles was ready to enter the school. The Head-Master at that time was, strangely enough, named Tait, spelt a little differently from the Richmond schoolmaster. Dr. Tait, who afterwards became Archbishop of Canterbury, was a most capable man, who governed the school for two of the three years that our Boy was a pupil. The last year, Dr. Goulburn was Head-Master.

Charles found Rugby a great change from the quiet of Richmond. He went up in February of 1846, the beginning of the second term, when football was in full swing. The teams practiced on the broad open campus known as "Big-side," and a "new boy" could only look on and applaud the great creatures who led the game. Rugby was swarming with boys—three hundred at least—from small fourteen-year-olders of the lowest "form," or class, to those of eighteen or twenty of the fifth and sixth, the highest forms. They treated little Dodgson in their big, burly, schoolboy fashion, hazed him to their hearts' content when he first entered, shrugging their shoulders good-naturedly over his love of study, in preference to the great games of cricket and football.

To have a fair glimpse of our Boy's life at this period, some little idea of Rugby and its surroundings might serve as a guide. Those who visit the school to-day, with its pile of modern, convenient, and ugly architecture, have no conception of what it was over sixty years ago, and even in 1846 it bore no resemblance to the original school founded by one Lawrence Sheriffe, "citizen and grocer of London" during the reign of Henry VIII. To begin with, it is situated in Shakespeare's own country, Warwickshire on the Avon River, and that in itself was enough to rouse the interest of any musing, bookish boy like Charles Dodgson.

From "Tom Brown's School Days," that ever popular book by Thomas Hughes, we may perhaps understand the feelings of the "new boy" just passing through the big, imposing school gates, with the oriel window above, and entering historic Rugby.

What first struck his view was the great school field or "close" as they called it, with its famous elms, and next, "the long line of gray buildings, beginning with the chapel and ending with the schoolhouse, the residence of the Head-Master where the great flag was lazily waving from the highest round tower."

As we follow *Tom Brown* through *his* first day, we can imagine our Boy's sensations when he found himself in this howling wilderness of boys. The eye of a boy is as keen as that of a girl regarding dress, and before *Tom Brown* was allowed to enter Rugby gates he was taken into the town and provided with a cat-skin cap, at seven and sixpence.

"'You see,' said his friend as they strolled up toward the school gates, in explanation of his conduct, 'a great deal depends on how a fellow cuts up at first. If he's got nothing odd about him and answers straightforward, and holds his head up, he gets on.'"

Having passed the gates, *Tom* was taken first to the matron's room, to deliver up his trunk key, then on a tour of inspection through the schoolhouse hall which opened into the quadrangle. This was "a great room, thirty feet long and eighteen high or thereabouts, with two great tables running the whole length, and two large fireplaces at the side with blazing fires in them."

This hall led into long dark passages with a fire at the end of each, and this was the hallway upon which the studies opened.

Now, to Charles Dodgson as well as to *Tom Brown*, a study conjured up untold luxury; it was in truth a "Rugby boy's citadel" usually six feet long and four feet broad. It was rather a gloomy light which came in through the bars and grating of the one window, but these precautions had to be taken with the studies on the ground floor, to keep the small boys from slipping out after "lock-up" time.

Under the window was usually a wooden table covered with green baize, a three-legged stool, a cupboard, and nails for hat and coat. The rest of the furnishings included "a plain flat-bottom candlestick with iron extinguisher and snuffers, a wooden candle-box, a staff-handle brush, leaden ink-pot, basin and bottle for washing the hands, and a saucer or gallipot for soap." There was always a cotton curtain or a blind before the window. For such a mansion the Rugby schoolboy paid from ten to fifteen shillings a year, and the tenant bought his own furniture. *Tom Brown* had a "hard-seated sofa covered with red stuff," big enough to hold two in a "tight squeeze," and he had, besides, a good, stout, wooden chair. Those boys who had looking-glasses in their rooms were able to comb their own locks, those who were not so fortunate went to what was known as the "combing-house" and had it done for them.

Unfortunately there are recorded very few details of these school-days at Rugby. We can only conjecture, from our knowledge of the boy and his studious ways, that Charles Dodgson's study was his castle, his home, and freehold while he was in the school. He drew around him a circle of friends, for the somewhat sober lad had the gift of talking, and could be jolly and entertaining when he liked.

The chapel at Rugby was an unpretentious Gothic building, very imposing and solemn to little Dodgson, who had been brought up in a most reverential way, but the Rugbeans viewed it in another light. *Tom Brown's* chosen chum explained it to him in this wise:

"That's the chapel you see, and there just behind it is the place for fights; it's most out of the way for masters, who all live on the other side and don't come by here after first lesson or callings-over. That's when the fights come off."

All this must have shocked the simple, law-abiding son of a clergyman. It took from four to six years to tame the average Rugby boy, but little Charles needed no discipline; he was not a "goody-goody" boy, he simply had a natural aversion to rough games and sports. He liked to keep a whole skin, and his mind clear for his studies; he was fond of tramping through the woods, or fishing along the banks of the pretty, winding Avon, or rowing up and down the river, or lying on some grassy slope, still weaving the many odd fancies which grew into clearer shape as the years passed. The boys at Rugby did not know he was a genius, he did not know it himself, happy little lad, just a bit quiet and old-fashioned, for the noisy, blustering life about him. In fact, strange as it may seem, Charles Dodgson was never really a little boy until he was quite grown up.

He easily fell in with the routine of the school, but discipline, even as late as 1846, was hard to maintain. The Head-Master had his hands full; there were six under-masters—one for each form—and special tutors for the boys who required them, and from the fifth and sixth forms, certain monitors were selected called "præposters," who were supposed to preserve order among the lower forms. In reality they bullied the smaller boys, for the system of fagging was much abused in those days, and the poor little fags had to be boot-blacks, water-carriers, and general servants to very hard task-masters, while the "præposter" had little thought of doing any service for the service he exacted; in fact the unfortunate fag had to submit in silence to any indignity inflicted by an older boy, for if by chance a report of such doings came to the ears of the Head-Master or his associates, the talebearer was "sent to Coventry," in other words, he was shunned and left to himself by all his companions.

Injustice like this made little Dodgson's blood boil; he submitted of course with the other small boys, but he always had a peculiar distaste for the life at Rugby. He owned several years later that none of the studying at Rugby was done from real love of it, and he specially bewailed the time he lost in writing out impositions, and he further confessed that under no consideration would he live over those three years again.

These "impositions" were the hundreds of lines of Latin or Greek which the boys had to copy out with their own hands, for the most trifling offenses—a weary and hopeless waste of time, with little good accomplished.

In spite of many drawbacks, he got on finely with his work, seldom returning home for the various holidays without one or more prizes, and we cannot believe that he was quite outside of all the fun and frolic of a Rugby schoolboy's life. For instance, we may be sure that he went bravely through that terrible ordeal for the newcomer, called "singing in Hall." "Each new boy," we are told, "was mounted in turn upon a table, a candle in each hand, and told to sing a song. If he made a false note, a violent hiss followed, and during the performance pellets and crusts of bread were thrown at boy or candles, often knocking them out of his hands and covering him with tallow. The singing over, he descended and pledged the house in a bumper of salt and water, stirred by a tallow candle. He was then free of the house and retired to his room, feeling very uncomfortable."

"On the night after 'new boys' night' there was chorus singing, in which solos and quartets of all sorts were sung, especially old Rugby's favorites such as:

"'It's my delight, on a shiny night
In the season of the year,'

and the proceedings always wound up with 'God save the Queen.'"

Guy Fawkes' Day was another well-known festival at Rugby. There were bonfires in the town, but they were never kindled until eight o'clock, which was "lock-up" time for Rugby school. The boys resented this as it was great fun and they were out of it, so each year there was a lively scrimmage between the Rugbeans and the town, the former bent on kindling the bonfires before "lock-up" time, the latter doing all they could to hold back the ever-pressing enemy. Victory shifted with the years, from one side to the other, but the boys had their fun all the same, which was over half the battle.

Charles must have gone through Rugby with rapid strides, accomplishing in three years' time what *Tom Brown* did in eight, and when he left he had the proud distinction of being among the *very* few who had never gone up a certain winding staircase leading, by a small door, into the Master's private presence, where the rod awaited the culprit, and a good heavy rod it was.

During these years Dickens was doing his best work, and while at Rugby, Charles read "David Copperfield," which came out in numbers in the *Penny Magazine*. He was specially interested in *Mrs. Gummidge*, that mournful, tearful lady, who was constantly bemoaning that she was "a lone lorn creetur," and that everything went "contrairy" with her. Dickens's humor touched a chord of sympathy in him, and if we go over in our minds, the weeping animals we know in "Alice in Wonderland" and "Through the Looking-Glass," we will find many excellent portraits of *Mrs. Gummidge*.

He also read Macaulay's "History of England," and from it was particularly struck by a passage describing the seven bishops who had signed the invitation to the Pretender. Bishop Compton,

one of the seven, when accused by King James, and asked whether he or any of his ecclesiastical brethren had anything to do with it, replied: "I am fully persuaded, your Majesty, that there is not one of my brethren who is not innocent in the matter as myself." This tickled the boy's sense of humor. Those touches always appealed to him; as he grew older they took even a firmer hold upon him and he was quick to pluck a laugh from the heart of things.

His life at Rugby was somewhat of a strain; with a brain beginning to teem with a thousand fairy fancies that the boys around him could not appreciate, he was forced to thrust them out of sight. He flung himself into his studies, coming out at examinations on top in mathematics, Latin, and divinity, and saving that other part of him for his sisters, when he went home for the holidays.

Meantime he continued to write verses and stories and to draw clever caricatures. There is one of these drawings peculiarly Rugbean in character; it is supposed to be a scene in which four of his sisters are roughly handling a fifth, because she *would* write to her brother when they wished to go to Halnaby and the Castle. This noble effort he signed "Rembrandt."

The picture is really very funny. The five girls have very much the appearance of the marionettes he was fond of making, especially the unfortunate correspondent who has been pulled into a horizontal position by the stern sister. The whole story is told by the expression of the eyes and mouth of each, for the clever schoolboy had all the secrets of caricature, without quite enough genius in that direction to make him an artist.

The Rugby days ended in glory; our Boy, no longer little Dodgson, but young Dodgson, came home loaded with honors. Mr. Mayor, his mathematical master, wrote to his father in 1848, that he had never had a more promising boy at his age, since he came to Rugby. Mr. Tait also wrote complimenting him most highly not only for his high standing in mathematics and divinity, but for his conduct while at Rugby, which was all that could be desired.

We can now see the dawning of the two great loves of his life, but there was another love, which Rugby brought forth in all its

beauty and strength, the love for girls. From that time he became their champion, their friend, and their comrade; whatever of youth and of boyhood was in his nature came out in brilliant flashes in their company. Boys, in his estimation, *had* to be, of course—a necessary evil, to be wrestled with and subdued. But girls—God bless 'em! were girls; that was enough for young Dodgson to the end of the chapter.

Chapter III

Home Life During the Holidays

Then Charles came home on his holiday visits, he was undoubtedly the busiest person at Croft Rectory. We must remember there were ten eager little brothers and sisters who wanted the latest news from "the front," meaning Rugby of course, and Charles found many funny things to tell of the school doings, many exciting matches to recount, many a thrilling adventure, and, alas! many a tale of some popular hero's downfall and disgrace. He had sketches to show, and verses to read to a most enthusiastic audience, the girls giggling over his funny tales, the boys roaring with excitement as in fancy they pictured the scene at "Big-side" during some great football scrimmage, for Charles's descriptions were so vivid, indeed he was such a good talker always, that a few quaint sentences would throw the whole picture on the canvas.

Vacation time was devoted to literary schemes of all kinds. From little boyhood until he was way up in his "teens," he was the editor of one magazine or another of home manufacture, chiefly, indeed, of his own composition, or drawn from local items of interest to the young people of Croft Rectory. While he was still at Richmond School, *Useful and Instructive Poetry* was born and died in six months' time, and many others shared the same fate; but the young editor was undaunted.

This was the age of small periodicals and he had caught the craze; it was also the age when great genius was burning brightly in England. Tennyson was in his prime; Dickens was writing his stories, and Macaulay his history of England. There were many other geniuses who influenced his later years, Carlyle, Browning and others, but the first three caught his boyish fancy and were his guides during those early days of editorship. *Punch*, the great English magazine of wit and humor, attracted him immensely, and many a time his rough drawings caught the spirit of some of the famous cartoons. He never imagined, as he laughed over the broad humor of John Tenniel, that the great cartoonist would one day stand beside him and share the honors of "Alice in Wonderland."

One of his last private efforts in the editorial line was *The Rectory Umbrella*, a magazine undertaken when he was about seventeen or eighteen years old, on the bridge, one might say, between boyhood and his approaching Oxford days. His mind had developed quickly, though his views of life did not go far beyond the rectory grounds. He evidently took his title out of the umbrella-stand in the rectory hall, the same stand doubtless which furnished him with "The Walking Stick of Destiny," a story of the lurid, exciting sort, which made his readers' hair rise. The magazine also contained a series of sketches supposed to have been copied from paintings by Rembrandt, Sir Joshua Reynolds and others whose works hang in the Vernon Gallery. One specially funny caricature of Sir Joshua Reynolds's "Age of Innocence" represents a baby hippopotamus smiling serenely under a tree not half big enough to shade him.

Another sketch ridicules homeopathy and is extremely funny. Homeopathy is a branch of medical science which believes in *very* small doses of medicine, and this picture represents housekeeping on a homeopathic plan; a family of six bony specimens are eating infinitesimal grains of food, which they can only see through the spectacles they all wear, and their table talk hovers round millionths and nonillionths of grains.

But the cleverest poem in *The Rectory Umbrella* is the parody on "Horatius," Macaulay's famous poem, which is supposed to be a true tale of his brothers' adventures with an obdurate donkey. It is the second of the series called "Lays of Sorrow," in imitation of Macaulay's "Lays of Ancient Rome," and the tragedy lies in the sad fact that the donkey succeeds in getting the better of the boys.

"Horatius" was a great favorite with budding orators of that day. The Rugby boys declaimed it on every occasion, and reading it over in these modern times of peace, one is stirred by the martial note in it. No wonder boys like Charles Dodgson loved Macaulay, and it is pretty safe to say that he must have had it by heart, to have treated it in such spirited style and with such pure fun. Indeed, fun bubbled up through everything he wrote; wholesome, honest fun, which was a safety valve for an over-serious lad.

This period was his halting time, and the humorous skits he dashed off were done in moments of recreation. He was mapping out his future in a methodical way peculiarly his own. Oxford was to be his goal, divinity and mathematics his principal studies, and he was working hard for his examinations. The desire of the eldest son to follow in his father's footsteps was strengthened by his own natural inclination, for into the boy nature crept a rare golden streak of piety. The reverence for holy things was a beautiful trait in his character from the beginning to the end of his life; it never pushed itself aggressively to the front, but it sweetened the whole of his intercourse with people, and was perhaps the secret of the wonderful power he had with children.

The intervening months between Rugby and Oxford were also the boundary-line between boyhood and young manhood, that most important period when the character shifts into a steadier pose, when the young eyes try vainly to pierce the mists of the future, and the young heart-throbs are sometimes very painful. Between those Rugby school-days and the more serious Oxford ones, something happened—we know not what—which cast a shadow on our Boy's life. He was young enough to live it down, yet old enough to feel keenly whatever sorrow crossed his path, and as he never married, we naturally suspect that some unhappy love affair, or death perhaps, had cut him off from all the joys so necessary to a young and deep-feeling man. Whatever it was—and he kept his own secret—it did not mar the sweetness of his nature, it did not kill his youth, nor deaden the keen wit which was to make the world laugh one day. It drew some pathetic lines upon his face, a wistful touch about mouth and eyes, as we can see in all his portraits.

A slight reserve hung as a veil between him and people of his own age, but it opened his heart all the wider to the children, whose true knight he became when, as "Lewis Carroll" he went forth to conquer with a laugh. We say "children," but we mean "girls." The little boy might just as well have been a caged animal at the Zoo, for all the notice he inspired. Of course, there were some younger brothers of his own to be considered, but he had such a generous provision of sisters that he didn't mind, and then, besides, one's own people are different somehow; we know well enough we wouldn't change *our* brothers and sisters for the finest little paragons that walk. So with Lewis Carroll; he strongly objected to everybody else's little brothers but his own, and it is even true that in later years there were some small nephews and boy cousins, to whom he was extremely kind. But as yet there is no Lewis Carroll, only a grave and earnest Charles Lutwidge Dodgson, reading hard to enter Christ Church, Oxford, that grand old edifice steeped in history, where his own father had "blazed a trail."

Mathematics absorbed many hours of each day, and Latin and Greek were quite as important. English as a "course" was not thought of as it is to-day; the classics were before everything else, although ancient and modern history came into use.

For lighter reading, Dickens was a never-failing source of supply. All during this holiday period "David Copperfield" was coming out in monthly instalments, and though the hero was "only a boy," there was something in the pathetic figure of lonely little *David*, irresistibly appealing to the young fellow who hated oppression and injustice of any kind, and was always on the side of the weak. While the dainty picture of *Little Em'ly* might have been his favorite, he was keenly alive to the absurdities of *Mrs. Gummidge*, the doglike devotion of *Peggotty*, and the horrors of the "cheap school," which turned out little shivering cowards instead of wholesome hearty English boys.

Later on, he visited the spot on which Dickens had founded *Dotheboys Hall* in "Nicholas Nickleby." "Barnard's Castle" was a most desolate region in Yorkshire. He tells of a trip by coach, over a land of dreary hills, into Bowes, a Godforsaken village where the original of *Dotheboys Hall* was still standing, though in a very dilapidated state, actually falling to pieces. As we well know, after the writing of "Nicholas Nickleby," government authorities began to look into the condition of the "cheap schools" and to remedy some of the evils. Even the more expensive schools, where the tired little brains were crammed to the brim until the springs were worn out and the minds were gone, were exposed by the great novelist when he wrote "Dombey and Son" and told of *Dr. Blimber's* school, where poor little *Paul* studied until his head grew too heavy for his fragile body. The victims of these three schools—*David, Smike, and Little Paul*—twined themselves about the heartstrings of the thoughtful young student, and many a humorous bit besides, in the works of Lewis Carroll, bears a decided flavor of those dips into Dickens.

Macaulay furnished a more solid background in the reading line. His history, such a complete chronicle of England from the fall of the Stuarts to the reign of Victoria, appealed strongly to the patriotism of the English boy, and the fact that Macaulay was not only a *writer* of English history, but at the same time a *maker* of history, served to strengthen this feeling.

If we compare the life of Lord Macaulay with the life of Lewis Carroll, we will see that there was something strangely alike about them. Both were unmarried, living alone, but with strong family ties which softened their lives and kept them from becoming crusty old bachelors. It is very probable, indeed, that the younger man modeled his life somewhat along the lines of the older, whom he greatly admired. Both were parts of great institutions; Macaulay stood out from the background of Parliament, as Lewis Carroll did from Oxford or more particularly Christ Church, and both names shone more brilliantly outside the routine of daily life.

But the influence that crept closer to the heart of this boy was that of Tennyson. The great poet with the wonderful dark face, the piercing eyes, the shaggy mane, sending forth clarion messages to the world in waves of song, was the inspiration of many a quaint phrase and poetic turn of thought which came from the pen of Lewis Carroll. For Tennyson became to him a thing of flesh and blood, a friend, and many a pleasant hour was spent in the poet's home in later years, when the fame of "Alice" had stirred his ambition to do other things. Many a verse of real poetry could trace its origin to association with the great man, who was quick to discover that there were depths in the soul of his young friend where genius dwelt.

Meantime Charles Dodgson read his poems over and over, in the seclusion of Croft Rectory, during that quiet pause in his life before he went up to Oxford.

There was a village school of some importance in Croft, and members of the Dodgson family were interested in its welfare, often lending a hand with the teaching, and during those months, no doubt, Charles took his turn. For society, his own family seemed to be sufficient. If he had any boy friends, there are no records of their intercourse; indeed, the only friend mentioned is T. Vere Bayne, who in childish days was his playfellow and who later became, like himself, a Student of Christ Church. This association cemented a lasting friendship. One or two Rugbeans claimed some intimacy, but his true friendships were formed when Lewis Carroll grew up and really became young.

Walking was always a favorite pastime; the woods were full of the things he loved, the wild things whose life stirred in the rustling of the leaves or the crackle of a twig, as some tiny animal whisked by. The squirrels were friendly, the hares lifted up their long ears, stared at him and scurried out of sight. Turtles and snails came out of the river to sun themselves on the banks; the air was full of the hum of insects and the chirp of birds.

As he lay under the friendly shelter of some great tree, he thought of this tree as a refuge for the teeming life about it; the beauty of its foliage, its spreading branches, were as nothing to its convenience as a home for the birds and chipmunks and the burrowing things that lived beneath its roots or in the hollows of its trunk.

These creatures became real companions in time. He studied their ways and habits, he looked them up in the Natural History, and noting their peculiarities, tucked them away in that quaint cupboard of his which he called his memory.

How many things were to come out of that cupboard in later days! He himself did not know what was hidden there. It reminded one of a chest which only a special key could open, and he did not even know there *was* a key, until on a certain "golden afternoon" he found it floating on the surface of the river. He grasped it, thrust it into the rusty lock, and lo!—but dear me, we are going too far ahead, for that is quite another chapter, and we have left Charles Dodgson lying under a tree, watching the lizards and snails and ants at their work or play, weaving his quaint fancies, dreaming perhaps, or chatting with some little sister or other who chanced to be with him. There was always a sister to chat with, which in part accounted for his liking for girls.

So, through a long vista of years, we have the picture of our Boy, between eighteen and nineteen, when he was about to put boyhood by forever and enter the stately ranks of the Oxford undergraduates. As he stands before us now, young, ardent, hopeful, and inexperienced, we can see no glimmer of the fairy wand which turned him into a wizard.

We see only a boy, somewhat old for his years, very manly in his ways, with a well-formed head, on which the clustering dark hair grew thick, a sensitive mouth and deep blue eyes, full of expression. He was clever, imitative, and consequently a good actor in the little plays he wrote and dramatized; he was very shy, but at his best in the home circle. He enjoyed nothing so much as an argument, always holding his ground with great obstinacy; a fine student, frank and affectionate, brimful of wit and humor, fond of reading, with a quiet determination to excel in whatever he undertook. With such weapons he was well equipped to "storm the citadel" at Oxford.

On May 23, 1850, he went up to matriculate—that is, to register his name and go through some examinations and the formality of becoming a student. Christ Church was to be his college, as it had been his father's before him. Archdeacon Dodgson was much gratified by the many letters he received congratulating him on the fact that he had a son worthy to succeed him, for he was well remembered in the college, where he had left a brilliant record behind him.

It certainly sounds a little queer to have the name of a church attached to one of the colleges of a university, but our colleges in America are comparatively so new that we cannot grasp the vastness and the antiquity of the great English universities. Under the shelter of Oxford, and covering an area of at least five miles, twenty colleges or more were grouped, each one a community in itself, and all under the rule of the Chancellor of Oxford. Christ Church received as students those most interested in the divinity courses, though in other respects the undergraduates could take up whatever studies they pleased, and Charles Dodgson put most of his energy into mathematics and the necessary study of the classics.

Seven months intervened between his matriculation and his real entrance into Oxford; these seven months we have just reviewed, full of study and pleasant family associations, with youthful experiments in literature, full of promise for the future—and something deeper still—which must have touched him just here, "where the brook and river meet."

Into all our lives at some time or other comes a solemn silence; it may spring from many causes, from a joy which cannot be spoken, or from a sorrow too deep for utterance, but it comes, and we cover it gently and hide it away, as something too sacred for the common light of every day.

This was the silence which came to Lewis Carroll on the threshold of his career; but lusty youth was with him as he stood before the portal of a brilliant future, and there was courage and high hope in his heart as he knocked for entrance.

Chapter IV

Oxford Scholarship and Honors

In January 24, 1851, just three days before his nineteenth birthday, Charles Dodgson took up his residence at Christ Church, and from that time to the day of his death his name was always associated with the fine old building which was his *Alma Mater*. The men of Christ Church called it the "House," and were very proud of their college, as well they might be, for Oxford could not boast of a more imposing structure. There is a great difference between a university and a college. A university is great enough to shelter many colleges, and its chancellor is ruler over all. When we reflect that Christ Church College, alone, included as many important buildings as are to be found in some of our modern American universities, we may have some idea of the extent of Oxford University, within whose boundaries twenty such colleges could be counted.

Their names were all familiar to the young fellow, and many a time, in those early days, he could be found in his boat upon the river, floating gently down stream, the whole panorama of Oxford spread out before him.

> "Now rising o'er the level plain,
> ' Mid academic groves enshrined.
> The Gothic tower, the Grecian fane,
> Ascend in solemn state combined."

The spire of St. Aldates (pronounced St. Olds); Sir Christopher Wren's domed tower over the entrance to Christ Church; the spires of the Cathedral of St. Mary; the tower of All Saints; the twin towers of All Souls; the dome of Radcliffe Library; the massive tower of Merton, and the beautiful pinnacles of Magdalen, all passed before him, "rising o'er the level plain" as the verse puts it, backed by dense foliage, and sharply outlined against the blue horizon.

History springs up with every step one takes in Oxford. The University can trace its origin to the time of Alfred the Great. Beginning with only three colleges, each year this great center of learning became more important. Henry I built the Palace of Beaumont at Oxford, because he wished frequent opportunities to talk with men of learning. It was from the Castle of Oxford that the Empress Maud escaped at dead of night, in a white gown, over the snow and the frozen river, when Stephen usurped the throne. It was in the Palace of Beaumont that Richard the Lion-Hearted was born, and so on, through the centuries, great deeds and great events could be traced to the very gates of Oxford.

But most of all, the young student's affections centered around Christ Church, and indeed, for the first few years of his college life, he had little occasion to go outside of its broad boundaries unless for a row upon the river.

Christ Church really owes its foundation to the famous Cardinal Wolsey. Charles Lutwidge Dodgson had its history by heart; how the wicked old prelate, wishing to leave behind him a monument of lasting good to cover his many misdeeds, obtained the royal license to found the college as early as 1525; how, in 1529, as Shakespeare said, he bade "a long farewell to all his greatness," and his possessions, including Cardinal College as it was then called, fell into the ruthless hands of Henry VIII; and how, after many ups and downs, the present foundation of Christ Church was created under "letters patent of Henry VIII dated November 4, 1546."

Christ Church, with its imposing front of four hundred feet, is built around the Great Quadrangle, quite famous in the history of the college. It includes in the embrace of its four sides the library and picture gallery, the Cathedral and the Chapter House, and the homes of the dean and his associates. There was another smaller quadrangle called Peckwater Quadrangle, where young Dodgson had his rooms when he first entered college, but later when he became a tutor or a "don" as the instructors were usually called, he moved into the Great Quadrangle. A beautiful meadow lies beyond the south gate, spreading out in a long and fertile stretch to the river's edge.

The massive front gate has towers and turrets on either side, while just above it is the great "Tom Tower," the present home of "Tom" the famous bell, measuring over seven feet in diameter and weighing over seven tons. This bell was originally dedicated to St. Thomas of Canterbury, and bore a Latin inscription in praise of the saint. It was brought from the famous Abbey of Oseney, when that cloister was transferred to Oxford, and on the accession of Queen Mary, the ruling dean rechristened it Mary, out of compliment to her; but this was not a lasting change; "Tom" was indeed the favored name. After "Bonnie Prince Charlie" came into his own, and Christopher Wren's tower was completed, the great bell was moved to the new resting place, where it rang first on the anniversary of the Restoration, May 29, 1684, and since then has rung each morning and evening, at the opening and closing of the college gates.

"Tom Tower," as it is called, overlooks that portion of the Great Quadrangle popularly known as "Tom Quad," and it was in this corner of the Great Quadrangle that Lewis Carroll had his rooms. He speaks of it often in his many reminiscences, as he also spoke of the new bell tower over the hall staircase in the southeast corner. This new tower was built to hold the twelve bells which form the famous Christ Church peal, some twenty years after his entrance as an undergraduate. This, and the new entrance to the cathedral from "Tom Quad," were designed by the architect, George Bodley, and Lewis Carroll, who was then a very dignified and retiring "don," ridiculed his work in a clever little booklet called "The Vision of the Three T's."

In it he calls the new tower the "Tea-chest," the passage to the cathedral the "Trench," the entrance itself the "Tunnel" (here we have the three T's). The architect, whose initials are G. B., he thinly disguises as "Jeeby," and his disapproval is expressed through "Our Willie," meaning William E. Gladstone, who gives vent to his rage in this fashion:

> "For as I'm true knight, a fouler sight,
> I'd never live to see.
> Before I'd be the ruffian dark,

Who planned this ghastly show,
I'd serve as secretary's clerk [pronounced *clark*]
To Ayrton or to Lowe.
Before I'd own the loathly thing,
That Christ Church Quad reveals,
I'd serve as shoeblack's underling
To Odger and to Beales."

But no thought of ridicule entered the earnest young scholar's mind during those early days at Oxford. Everything he saw in his surroundings was most impressive. There was much about the college routine to remind him of the old Rugby days. Indeed, it was not so very long before his time that the birch-rod was laid aside in Oxford; the rules were still very strict, and the student was forced to work hard to gain any standing whatever.

Young Dodgson went into his studies, as he did into everything else, with his whole soul. He devoted a great deal of his time to mathematics, and quite as much to divinity, but just as he had settled down for months of serious work, the news of his mother's sudden death sent him hurrying back to Croft Rectory to join the sorrowing household. It was a terrible blow to them all; with this young family growing up around her, she could ill be spared, and the loss of her filled those first Oxford days with dark shadows for the boy—he was only a boy still for all his nineteen years—and we can imagine how deeply he mourned for his mother.

What we know of her is very faint and shadowy. That her influence was keenly felt for many years, we can only glean from the love and reverence with which the memory of her was guarded; for this English home hid its grief in the depths of its heart, and only the privileged few might enter and console.

This was the first and only break in the family for many years. Charles went back to Oxford immediately after the funeral, and took up his studies again with redoubled zeal.

Thomas Gaisford was dean of Christ Church during the four years that Charles Dodgson was an undergraduate. He was a most able man, well known as scholar, writer, and thinker, but he died, much lamented, in 1855, just as the young student was thinking seriously of a life devoted to his college. George Henry Liddell came into residence as dean of Christ Church, an office which he held for nearly forty years, and as Dean Liddell stood for a great deal in the life of Charles Dodgson, we shall hear much of him from time to time, dating more especially from the comradeship of his three little daughters, who were the first "really truly" friends of Lewis Carroll.

But we are jumping over too many years at once, and must go back a few steps. His hard study during the first year won him a Boulter scholarship; the next year he took First Class honors in mathematics, and a second in classical studies, and on Christmas Eve, 1852, he was made a Student of Christ Church College.

To become a Student of Christ Church was not only a great honor, conferred only on one altogether worthy of it, but it was a very serious step in life for a young man. A Student remained unmarried and always took Holy Orders; he was of course compelled to be very regular at chapel service, and to be devoted, heart and soul, to the interests of Christ Church, all of which this special young Student had no difficulty in following to the letter.

From that time forth he ordered his life as he planned his mathematics, clearly and simply, and once his career was settled, Charles Lutwidge Dodgson dropped from his young shoulders— he was only twenty—the mantle of over-seriousness, and looked about for young companionship. He found what he needed in the households of the masters and the tutors, whose homes looked out upon the Great Quadrangle. Here on sunny days the nurses brought the children for an airing; chubby little boys in long trousers and "roundabouts," dainty little girls, with corkscrew ringlets and long pantalets and muslin "frocks" and poke bonnets, in the depths of which were hidden the rosebud faces. These were the favorites of the young Student, whose slim figure in cap and gown was often the center of an animated group of tiny girls; one on his lap, one perhaps on his shoulder, several at his knee, while he told them stories of the animals he knew, and drew funny little pictures on stray bits of paper. The "roundabouts" went to the wall: they were only boys!

His coming was always hailed with delight. Sometimes he would take them for a stroll, always full of wonder and interest to the children, for alone, with these chosen friends of his, his natural shyness left him, the sensitive mouth took smiling curves, the deep blue eyes were full of laughter, and he spun story after story for them in his quaint way, filling their little heads with odd fancies which would never have been there but for him. The "bunnies" held animated conversations with these small maids; every chirp and twitter of the birds grew to mean something to them. He took them across the meadow, and showed them the turtles swimming on the river bank; sometimes even—oh, treat of treats!—he took them in his boat, and pulling gently down the pretty rippling stream, told them stories of the shining fish they could see darting here and there in its depths, and of wonderful creatures they could *not* see, who would not show themselves while curious little girls were staring into the water.

These were hours of pure recreation for him. The small girls could not know what genuine pleasure they gave; the young undergraduates could never understand his lack of sympathy with their many sports. Athletics never appealed to him, even boating he enjoyed in his own mild way; a quiet pull up or down the river, a shady bank, an hour's rest under the trees, a companion perhaps, generally some small girl, whose round-eyed interest inspired some remarkable tale—this was what he liked best. On other days a tramp of miles gave just the exercise he needed.

His busy day began at a quarter past six, with breakfast at seven, and chapel at eight. Then came the day's lectures in Greek and Latin, mathematics, divinity, and the classics.

Meals were served to the undergraduates in the Hall. The men were divided into "messes" just as in military posts; each "mess" consisted of about six men, who were served at a small table. There were many such tables scattered over the Hall, a vast and ancient room, completed at the time of Wolsey's fall, 1529, an interesting spot full of memorials of Henry VIII and Wolsey. The great west window with its two rows of shields, some with a Cardinal's hat, others with the royal arms of Henry VIII, is most interesting, while the wainscoting, decorated with shields also arranged in orderly fashion, is very attractive. The Hall is filled with portraits of celebrities, from Henry VIII, Wolsey and Elizabeth to the many students, and famous deans, who have added luster to Christ Church.

In Charles Dodgson's time, the meals were poorly served. The Hall was lighted at night with candles in brass candlesticks made to hold three lights each. The undergraduates were served on pewter plates, and the poor young fellows were in the hands of the cook and butler, and consequently were cheated up to their eyes. They did not complain in Charles Dodgson's time, but after he graduated and became a master himself he no doubt took part in what was known as the "Bread and Butter" campaign, when the undergraduates rose up in a body and settled the cook and butler for all time, appointing a steward who could overlook the doings of those below in the kitchen.

This kitchen is a very wonderful old place, the first portion of Wolsey's work to be completed, and so strongly was it built, and so well has it lasted, that it seems scarcely to have been touched by time. Of course there are some modern improvements, but the great ranges are still there, and the wide fireplace and spits worked by a "smoke jack." Wolsey's own gridiron hangs just above the fireplace, a large uncouth affair, fit for cooking the huge hunks of meat the Cardinal liked best.

We must not imagine that the years at Oxford were "all work and no play," for Charles Dodgson's many vacations were spent either at home, where his father made much of him, his brothers looked up to him, and his sisters petted and spoiled him, or on little trips of interest and amusement.

Once, during what is known as the "Long Vacation," he visited London at the time of the Great Exhibition, and wrote a vivid letter of description to his sister Elizabeth. What seemed to interest him most was the vastness of everything he saw, the huge crystal fountain and the colossal statues on either side of the central aisle. One statue he particularly noticed. It was called the "Amazon and the Tiger," and many of us have doubtless seen the picture, the strong, erect, girlish figure on horseback, and the tiger clinging to the horse, his teeth buried in his neck, the girl's face full of terror, the horse rearing with fright and pain. He always liked anything that told a story, either in statues or in pictures, and in after years, when he became a skilled photographer, he was fond of taking his many girlfriends in costume, for somehow it always suggested a story.

He was also very fond of the theater, and he made many a trip to London to see a special play. Shakespeare was his delight, and "Henry VIII" was certainly the most appropriate play for a Student of Christ Church College to see. The great actor, Charles Kean, took the part of *Cardinal Wolsey*, and Mrs. Kean shone forth as poor *Queen Katharine*, the discarded wife of Henry VIII. What impressed him most was the vision of the sleeping queen, the troops of floating angels with palm branches in their hands, which they waved slowly over her, while shafts of light fell upon them from above. Then as the Queen awoke they vanished, and raising her arms she called "Spirits of peace, where are ye?" Poor Queen, no wonder her audience shed tears! Henry VIII was not an easy man to get along with, even in his sweetest mood!

In 1854, Charles Dodgson began hard study for final examinations, working sometimes as many as thirteen hours a day during the last three weeks, but the subjects which he had to prepare were philosophy and history, neither of which were special favorites, and though he passed fairly well, his name was not among the first.

During the following Long Vacation he went to Whitby, where he prepared for final examination in mathematics, and so well did he work that he took First Class honors and became quite a distinguished personage among the undergraduates. His prowess in so difficult a subject traveled even beyond the college walls, and congratulations poured in upon him until he laughingly declared that if he had shot the Dean there could not have been more commotion. This meant a great deal to him; to begin with, he stood head on the list of five very able men who were close to him in the marking. He came out number 279 and the lowest of the five was 213, so it was a hard fight in a hard subject, and Lewis Carroll might be forgiven for a little quiet "bragging" in the letter he wrote his father, telling the result of the examinations. Of one thing he was now quite sure—a future lectureship in Christ Church College.

On December 18, 1854, he graduated, taking the degree of Bachelor of Arts, and the following year, October 15, 1855, to celebrate the appointment of Dean Liddell, he was made a "Master of the House," meaning that under the roof of Christ Church College he had all the privileges of a Master of Arts, which is the next higher degree; but he did not become a Master of Arts in the University until two years later. When a college graduate puts B.A. after his name, we know that means Bachelor of Arts, the first college degree, and M.A. means Master of Arts, the second degree.

The young Student was glad to be free of college restraint and to begin work. Archdeacon Dodgson was not a rich man, and though his son had never faced the trials of poverty, he was anxious to become independent. Now that the "grinding" study was over, his thoughts turned fondly to a literary life. His numerous clever sketches, too, gave him hope of better work hereafter, and this we know had been his dream through his boyish years; it was his dream still, but where his talent would lie he had no idea, though hazy poems and queer jumbles of words popped into his mind on the slightest notice. Still he could not settle down seriously to such work just at first; there was other work at hand and he must learn to wait. During the first year of tutorship he took many private pupils, besides lecturing in mathematics, his chosen profession, from three to three and a half hours a day. The next year he was one of the regular lecturers, and often lectured seven hours a day, not counting the time it took him to prepare his work.

Mathematicians are born, not made; this young fellow had not only the power of solving problems, but the rare gift of being able to teach others to solve them also, and many a student has been heard to declare that mathematics was never a dull study with Mr. Dodgson to explain. We can imagine the slight, youthful figure of the young college "don," his clean-cut, refined face, full of light and interest, his blue eyes flashing as he tackled some difficult problem, wrestled with it before his class in the lecture-hall, and undid the tangle without the slightest trouble.

He "took to" problems as naturally as a duck to water; the harder they were the more resolutely he bent to his task. Sometimes the tussle kept him awake half the night, often he was up at dawn to renew the battle, but he usually "won out," and this is what made him so good a teacher—he *never* "let go." Whatever mathematical ax he had to grind, he always managed to put a keen edge upon it sooner or later.

To his many friends, especially his many girl friends, this side of his character was most remarkable. How this fun-making, fun-loving, story-telling nonsense rhymer could turn in a twinkling into the grave, precise "don" and discourse on rectangles, and polygons, and parallel lines, and unknown quantities was more than they could understand.

Girls, the best of them, the rarest and finest of them, are not, as a rule, fond of mathematics. They "take" it in school, as they "take" whooping cough and measles at home, but in those days they seldom went further than the "first steps" in plain arithmetic. Girls, especially the little girls of Charles Dodgson's immediate circle, rarely went to school; they were usually in the care of governesses who helped them along the narrow path of learning which they themselves had trod, and these little maids could truly say, with all their hearts:

> "Multiplication is vexation,
>
> Division is as bad,
>
> The Rule of Three, it puzzles me,
>
> And Fractions drive me mad!"

It was certainly thought quite unnecessary to educate girls in higher mathematics; those were not the days when colleges for girls were thought of. The little daughters of the wise Oxford men were considered finely grounded if they had mastered the three

R's—("Reading, 'Riting, and 'Rithmetic") and the young "don" knew pretty well how far they were led along these paths, for if we remember our "Alice in Wonderland" we may easily recall that interesting conversation between *Alice*, the *Mock Turtle* and the *Gryphon*, about schools, the *Mock Turtle* remarking with a sigh:

"I took only the regular course."

"What was that?" inquired Alice.

"Reeling and Writhing, of course, to begin with," the Mock Turtle replied, "and then the different branches of Arithmetic— Ambition, Distraction, Uglification, and Derision."

"What else had you to learn?" asks Alice later on.

"Well, there was Mystery," the Mock Turtle replied, counting off the subjects on his flappers, "Mystery—ancient and modern—with Seography; then Drawling—the Drawling-master was an old Conger-eel that used to come once a week; *he* taught us Drawling, Stretching, and Fainting in Coils." [Drawing, sketching, and painting in oils.] Lewis Carroll loved this play upon words.

"What was *that* like?" said Alice.

"Well, I can't show it you myself," the Mock Turtle said, "I'm too stiff. And the Gryphon never learnt it."

"Hadn't time," said the Gryphon. "I went to the Classical master though. He was an old Crab, *he* was."

"I never went to him," the Mock Turtle said, with a sigh; "he taught Laughing and Grief, they used to say."

"So he did, so he did," said the Gryphon, sighing in his turn, and both creatures hid their faces in their paws.

It is doubtful if any little girl in Lewis Carroll's time ever learned "Laughing and Grief" unless she was *very* ambitious, but many a quick, active young mind absorbed the simple problems which he was constantly turning into games for them.

So the years passed over the head of this young Student of Christ Church. They were pleasantly broken by long vacations at Croft Rectory, by trips through the beautiful English country, by one special journey to the English lakes, where Wordsworth, Southey, and Coleridge lived and wrote their poems. These trips were often afoot, and Charles Dodgson was very proud of the long distances he could tramp, no matter what the wind or the weather. There was nothing he liked better unless it was the occasional visits he made to the Princess's Theatre in London.

On June 16, 1856, he records seeing "A Winter's Tale," where he was specially pleased with little Ellen Terry, a beautiful tiny creature, who played the child's part of *Mamillius* in the most charming way. This was the first of many meetings with the famous actress, who became one of his child-friends in later years. But that was when he was Lewis Carroll. As yet he was only Charles Dodgson, a struggling young Student, anxious for independence, interested in his work, simple, sincere, devout, a dreamer of dreams which had not yet taken shape, and above all, a true lover of little girls, no matter how plain, or fretful, or rumpled, or even dirty. His kindly eyes could see beneath the creases on the top, his gentle fingers clasped the shrinking, trembling little hands; his low voice charmed them all unconsciously, and no doubt the children he loved did for him as much as he did for them. If he felt the strain of overwork nothing soothed him like a romp with his favorites, and young as he was, when dreaming of the future and the magic circle in which he would write his name, it was not of the great world he was thinking, but of bright young faces, with dancing eyes and sunny curls, and eager voices continually demanding—"One more story."

Chapter V

A Many-Sided Genius

We have traveled over the years with some speed, from the time that little Charles Lutwidge Dodgson was christened by his proud papa to the moment when the same proud father heard that his eldest son was made a student of Christ College—a good large slice out of a birthday-cake—twenty candles—if one counts birthdays by candles. It's a charming old German fashion, for the older one grows the brighter the lights become, and if you chance to get real old—a fine "threescore and ten"—why, if there's a candle for each year, there you are—in a perfect blaze of glory!

We have just passed over the very oldest part of our Boy's life; from the time he became Lewis Carroll, Charles Dodgson began to go backward; he did a lot of things backward, as we shall see later. He wrote letters backward, he told stories backward, he spelled and counted backward—in fact, he was so fond of doing things backward we do not wonder that he stepped out from the circle of the years, and turned backward to find the boyhood he had somehow missed before. This is when Lewis Carroll was born; but that is a story in itself.

Outwardly the life of the young Student seemed unchanged, but that is all we mortals know about it; the fairies were already at work. In moments of leisure little poems went forth to the world—a world which at first consisted of Croft Rectory—for there was another and last family magazine, of which he was sole editor and composer. He named it *Misch-Masch*, a curious old German word, which in our English means Hodge-Podge, and everybody, young and old, knows what a jumble Hodge-Podge is—something like New England succotash.

Misch-Masch was started by this enterprising young editor during the year after his graduation. He had become a person of vast experience between *Misch-Masch* and the days of *The Rectory Umbrella*, having been editor of *College Rhymes*, his college paper. He also wrote stories for the *Oxonian Advertiser* and the *Whitby Gazette*, and this printed matter, together with many new and original ideas and drawings, found a place in his new home venture.

His mathematical genius blossomed forth in a wonderful labyrinth or maze, a geometrical design within a given square form, of a tangle of intersecting lines and angles containing a hidden pathway to the center. These designs, that seem so remarkable to outsiders, were very simple to the editor of *Misch-Masch*, who was always inventing puzzles of some sort.

He also wrote a series of "Studies from the English Poets," which he illustrated himself. One specially good drawing was of the following line from one of Keats's poems. "She did so—but 'tis doubtful how or whence." The picture represents a very fat old lady, with a capitally drawn placid face, perched on a post marked "*Dangerous*," seemingly in midwater. In her chubby hand is a basket with the long neck of a goose hanging out.

Mr. Stuart Collingwood, Lewis Carroll's nephew, gives a most interesting account of these early editorial efforts, in an article written for the *Strand*, an English magazine. Speaking of the above illustration he says:

"Keats is the author whom our artist has honored, and surely the shade of that much neglected songster owes something to a picture which must popularize one passage at least in his works.

"The only way I can account for the lady's hazardous position is by supposing her to have attempted to cross a frozen lake after a thaw has set in. The goose, whose long neck projects from her basket, proves that she has just returned from market; probably the route across the lake was her shortest way home. We are to suppose that for some time she proceeded without any knowledge of the risk she was running, when suddenly she felt the ice giving way under her. By frantic exertions she succeeded in reaching the notice-board, to which she clung for days and nights together, till the ice was all melted and a deluge of rain caused the water to rise so many feet that at last she was compelled for dear life to climb to the top of the post." We can now understand how well the illustration fits in with the line:

"She did so, but 'tis doubtful how or whence."

Mr. Collingwood continues:

"Whether she sustained life by eating raw goose is uncertain. At least she did not follow Father William's example by devouring the beak. The question naturally suggests itself: Why was she not rescued? My answer is that either such a dense fog enveloped the whole neighborhood that even her bulky form was invisible, or that she was so unpopular a character that each man feared the hatred of the rest if he should go to her succor."

Mr. Collingwood concludes his article with the following riddle which the renowned editor of *Misch-Masch* presented to his readers; there must be an answer, and it is therefore worth while guessing, for Lewis Carroll would never have written a riddle without one:

> A monument, men all agree—
>> Am I in all sincerity;
> Half-cat, half-hindrance made
>> If head and tail removed shall be
> Then, most of all you strengthen me.
>> Replace my head—the stand you see
> On which my tail is laid.

Misch-Masch had a short but brilliant career, for magazines with a wider circulation than Croft Rectory began to claim his attention. *The Comic Times* was a small periodical very much on the order of *Punch*. Edmund Yates was the editor, and among the writers and artists were some of the best known in England. Charles Dodgson's poetry and sketches were too clever to hide themselves from public view, and he became a regular contributor.

Later, *The Comic Times* changed hands, and the old staff started a new magazine called *The Train*, in 1856, and the quiet Oxford "don" found his poetry in such demand that after talking it over with the editor, he decided to adopt a suitable pen name. He first suggested "Dares" in compliment to his birthplace, Daresbury, but the editor preferred a *real* name. Then he took his first two names, Charles Lutwidge, and transposing them he got two names, Edgar Cuthwellis or Edgar U. C. Westhill, neither of which sounded in the least interesting. Finally he decided to take the two names and look at them backward—this very queer young fellow always preferred to look at things backward—Lutwidge Charles. That was certainly not promising. Then he took one name at a time and analyzed it in his own quaint way. Lutwidge was surely derived from the Latin word Ludovicus—which in good sound English meant Lewis—ah, that was not bad! Now for Charles. Its Latin equivalent was Carolus— which could be easily changed in Carroll. The whole thing worked out like one of his own word puzzles, and Lewis Carroll he was, henceforth, whenever he made his appearance in print.

There was not much ceremony at *this* christening. Just two clever men put their heads together and the result was—Lewis Carroll! Charles Lutwidge Dodgson retired to his rooms at Christ Church College, where he prepared his lectures on mathematics and wrote the most learned text-books for the University; but Lewis Carroll peeped out into the world, which he found full of light and laughter and happy childhood, and as Lewis Carroll he was known to that world henceforth.

The first poem to appear with his new name was called "The Path of Roses," a very solemn, serious poem about half a yard long and not specially interesting, save as a contribution to a most inter-esting little paper. *The Train* was really very ambitious, full, indeed, of the best talent of the day. There were short stories and serials, poems, timely articles, jokes, puns, anecdates—in short, all the attractions that help toward the making of an attractive magazine, and though the illustrations were nothing but old-fashioned woodcuts, the reading was quite as good, and in many cases better than what we find in the average magazine of to-day.

Many of the little poems Lewis Carroll wrote at this time he tucked away in some cubby-hole and made use of later in one or the other of his books. One of his very earliest printed bits is called:

MY FANCY

I painted her a gushing thing,
　With years perhaps a score,
I little thought to find they were
　At least a dozen more.
My fancy gave her eyes of blue,
　A curly auburn head;
I came to find the blue—a green,
　The auburn turned to red.

She boxed my ears this morning,
　They tingled very much;
I own that I could wish her
　A somewhat lighter touch.
And if you were to ask me how
　Her charms might be improved,
I would not have them added to,
　But just a few removed!

She has the bear's ethereal grace,
　The bland hyena's laugh,
The footstep of the elephant,
　The neck of the giraffe;
I love her still, believe me,
　Tho' my heart its passion hides—
"She is all my fancy painted her,"
　But, oh—how much besides!

The quoted line—"She is all my fancy painted her"—is the line upon which he built the poem; he was very fond of doing this, and though no special mention is made of the fact, it is highly probable that these three telling verses found their way into *Misch-Masch*, among the "Studies from the Poets." It is unfortunate, too, that we have not some funny drawing of this wonderful "gushing thing" of the giraffe neck, "the bear's ethereal grace," and the "footstep of the elephant," for Lewis Carroll's drawings generally followed his thoughts; a pencil and bit of paper were always ready in some inner pocket, for illustrating purposes, and it is doubtful if any celebrated artist could produce more sketches on such a variety of subjects. His power to make his pencil "talk" impressed his sisters and brothers greatly; they caught every scrap of paper that fluttered from his hands, treasured it, and if the drawing was distinct enough, they colored it with crayons or touched it up in black and white, for the use of *The Rectory Umbrella* and the later publication of *Misch-Masch*. In his secret soul he longed to be an artist; he certainly possessed genius of a queer sort. A few strokes would tell the story, usually a funny one or a quaint one, but all his art failed to make his people look quite real or natural—just dolls stuffed with sawdust. But they were fine caricatures, and the young artist had to content himself with this smaller talent.

The Train published many of his poems during 1856-57. "Solitude," "Novelty and Romancement," "The Three Voices," followed one another in quick succession, but the best of all was decidedly "Hiawatha's Photographing," and this for more reasons than one. In the first place, from the time he went into residence at Christ Church photography was his great delight; he "took" people whenever he could—canons, deacons, deans, students, undergraduates and children. The "grown-ups" submitted with a gentle sort of patience, but he made his camera such a point of attraction for the youngsters that he could "take" them as often as he liked, and he has left behind him a wonderful array of photographs, many of well-known, even celebrated people, among whom we may find Tennyson, the Rossetti family, Ellen and Kate Terry, John Ruskin, George Macdonald, Charlotte M. Yonge, Sir John Millais, and many others known to fame; and considering that photography had not reached its present perfection, Lewis Carroll's photographs show remarkable skill. He would not have been Lewis Carroll if he had not gone into this fascinating pastime with his whole soul. Whenever he met a new face which interested him, we may be sure it was not long before the busy camera was at work. There is no doubt that his admiring family suffered agonies in posing, to say nothing of his friends who were not always beautiful enough to produce "pretty pictures"; their criticisms were often based entirely on their disappointment: hence the poem,

HIAWATHA'S PHOTOGRAPHING

[*With no apology to Mr. Longfellow.*]

From his shoulder Hiawatha
Took the camera of rosewood,
Made of sliding, folding rosewood;
Neatly put it all together,
In its case it lay compactly,
Folded into nearly nothing;
But he opened out the hinges,
Pushed and pulled the joints and hinges
Till it looked all squares and oblongs,
Like a complicated figure
In the second book of Euclid.

This he perched upon a tripod—
Crouched beneath its dusky cover—
Stretched his hand, enforcing silence—
Said, "Be motionless, I beg you!"
Mystic, awful was the process.
All the family in order
Sat before him for their pictures:
Each in turn, as he was taken,
Volunteered his own suggestions,
His ingenious suggestions.

All of which during the course of the poem succeeded in driving poor Hiawatha to the verge of madness, until—

Finally my Hiawatha
Tumbled all the tribe together
("Grouped" is not the right expression),

And, as appy chance would have it,
Did at last obtain a picture
Where the faces all succeeded:
Each came out a perfect likeness.

Then they joined and all abused it,
Unrestrainedly abused it,
As "the worst and ugliest picture
They could possibly have dreamed of."

. . . .

All together rang their voices,
Angry, loud, discordant voices,
As of dogs that howl in concert,
As of cats that wail in chorus.

But my Hiawatha's patience,
His politeness and his patience,
Unaccountably had vanished,
And he left that happy party.
Neither did he leave them slowly,
With the calm deliberation,
The intense deliberation,
Of a photographic artist:
But he left them in a hurry,
Left them in a mighty hurry,
Stating that he would not stand it,
Stating in emphatic language

What he'd be before he'd stand it.
Hurriedly he packed his boxes:
Hurriedly the porter trundled
On a barrow all his boxes:
Hurriedly he took his ticket:
Hurriedly the train received him:
Thus departed Hiawatha.

But perhaps the cleverest part of the poem is theseemingly innocent paragraph of introduction which reads as follows:

"In an age of imitation, I can claim no special merit for this slight attempt at doing what is known to be so easy. Any fairly practiced writer, with the slightest ear for rhythm, could compose, for hours together, in the easy running meter of 'The Song of Hiawatha.' Having, then, distinctly stated that I challenge no attention in the following little poem to its merely verbal jingle, I must beg the candid reader to confine his criticism to its treatment of the subject."

Notice how metrically this sounds. Tune up to the Hiawatha pitch and you will have the same swinging measure in the above sentences.

Lewis Carroll's real acquaintance with Tennyson began in that eventful year of 1856. The odd, shaggy man, with the fine head and the keen, restless eyes, fascinated the young Student greatly. He went often to Tennyson's home and did his best to be interested in the poet's two little boys, Hallam and Lionel. Had they been girls there would have been no difficulty, but he always had strained relations with boys; still, as these "roundabouts" belonged to the little Tennysons, we find a sort of armed truce kept up between them. He bargained with Lionel to exchange manuscripts, and he got both boys to sign their names in his album; he even condescended to play a game of chess with Lionel, checkmating him in six moves, but he distinctly refused to allow that young gentleman to give him a blow on the head with a mallet in exchange for some of his verses. However, we may be pretty sure that Lewis Carroll's visits to the Tennysons were much pleasanter when the "roundabouts" were not visible.

That same year he made the acquaintance of John Ruskin, and the great art critic turned out to be a very valuable friend, as was also Sir James Paget, the eminent surgeon, who gave him many hints on medicine and surgery, in which Charles Dodgson was deeply interested. His medical knowledge was quite remarkable, and the books he collected on the subject would have been valuable additions to any physician's library. In the year 1857 he met Thackeray, who had come to Oxford to deliver his lecture on George III, and liked him very much. The Oxford "dons" were certainly fortunate in meeting all the "great ones" and seeing them generally at their best.

The year 1858 was an uneventful year; college routine varied by much reading, afternoons on the river or in the country, and evenings devoted to preparations for the morrow's work. Lewis Carroll kept a diary which harbored many fine thoughts and noble resolves, many doubts and fears, many hopes, many plans for the future, for he was making up his mind to the final step in the life of a Christ Church Student—that of taking Holy Orders, in other words, of being ordained as a clergyman.

There were one or two points to be considered: first, regarding an impediment in his speech which would make constant preaching almost impossible. He stammered, not on all occasions, but quite enough to make steady speaking an effort, painful to himself and his hearers. The other objection lay in the fact that Christ Church had rigid laws for its clergy concerning amusements. Charles Dodgson had no wish to be shut out of the world; he was fond of theaters and operas, and he did not see that he was doing any special good to his fellow-creatures by putting them out of his life. But at last, after battling with his conscience, and earnest consultation with a few wise friends, he decided that he would be ordained, though he would not become a regular preaching clergyman.

It took him two years to reach this decision, for he was slow to act on such occasions, but strong of purpose when the step was taken. On October 17, 1859, the young Prince of Wales (the late King Edward VII) came into residence at Christ Church College. This was a mark of special favor to Dean Liddell, who had for many years been chaplain to Queen Victoria and her husband, the Prince Consort. Of course there was much ceremony attending the arrival of his Royal Highness; the Dean went in person to the station to meet him, and all the "dons" were drawn up in a body in Tom Quadrangle to give him the proper sort of greeting. "Hiawatha" had his camera along—"in its case it lay compactly," but his poor little Highness had been "served up" on the camera to his utter disgust, and nothing would induce him to be photographed.

Later in the season, the Queen, the Prince Consort, and several princes and princesses came up to Oxford and surprised everybody. Christ Church was certainly in a flutter, and the day was turned into a gala occasion. There was a brilliant reception that evening at Dean Liddell's and *tableaux vivants*, to which we may be sure our modest Lewis Carroll gave much assistance. He was already on intimate terms with the three little Liddells, Lorina, Alice, and Edith, and as the children were to pose in a tableau, he was certainly there to help and suggest with a score of quaint ideas.

He had a pleasant talk with the Prince of Wales, who shook hands cordially and condescended to ask several questions of the young photographer, praising the photographs which he had seen, and promised to choose some for himself some day. He regarded the pleasant-looking, chatty young fellow as just one of the college "dons"; he had never even heard of Lewis Carroll, indeed that gentleman was too newly born to be known very well anywhere outside of Charles Lutwidge Dodgson's study, and it is extremely doubtful if the grave Student himself knew of half the fun and merriment hidden away in the new name. As a result of his interview with the prince, Lewis Carroll obtained his autograph, which was quite a gem among his collection.

There is no doubt he had many fine autographs and also an album, as he mentions several times. Autograph-hunting was not carried to the excess that it was later on, and is to-day. It is, to put it mildly, a very bad habit. Total strangers have no hesitancy in asking this favor of celebrities, who, as a rule, object to the wholesale signing of their names.

But the signatures in Lewis Carroll's album were those of friends, which was quite another matter, and it was consequently most interesting to turn the leaves of the precious volume, and see in what friendly esteem he was held by the foremost men and women of his time. To him a letter or a sentiment would have had no meaning nor value if not addressed personally to himself; whereas, the autograph fiend of the present day would be content with the signature no matter to whom addressed. Lewis Carroll suffered from these pests in later years, as well as from the photograph fiend, to him as malicious as a hornet, and from whom he fled in terror.

Yet we find many good pictures of him, notwithstanding, the one which we have chosen for our frontispiece being the youngest and most attractive—Lewis Carroll at the age of twenty-three. There is another taken some two years later, when the dignity of the Oxford "don" set well on the slim young figure. His face was always curiously youthful in expression: the eyes, deep blue, looked childlike in their innocent trust; a child had but to gaze into their depths and claim a friend. Little girls, particularly, remembered their beauty, for they felt a thrill at their youthful heartstrings when those eyes, brimful of kindliness, turned upon them and warmed their childish souls. They were quick to feel the gentle pressure of his hand, his touch upon their shoulders or on their heads, which drew these little magnets close to his side where he loved to have them, for behind the shyness and reserve of Lewis Carroll was a great wealth of tenderness and love which only his girl friends understood, because it was only to them that he cared to show this part of himself.

Of course in his own home this side of him expanded in the sunny companionship of seven younger sisters. Naturally they did not look upon him with the awe of the later generation, but they brought to the surface many winning characteristics which might never have come to light but for them.

It had been his delight from early boyhood to tackle problems and to solve them; the "girl problem" he had studied from the very beginning, in all its stages, and so it is small wonder that he knew girls quite as well as he did mathematics, and loved them even better, if the truth must be told, though they were often quite as puzzling.

On December 22, 1861, in spite of many doubts and misgivings as to his worthiness, Charles Dodgson was ordained deacon by the Bishop of Oxford. He did this partly from his duty as a Student of Christ Church, but more because of the influence it would give him among the undergraduates, whose welfare he had so much at heart. He preached often but he never became a regular officiating clergyman, and his sermons were always delightful because they were never what we call "preachy."

He was so truly good and religious, his faith was so simple, his desire to do right was so unfailing, that in spite of the slight drawback in his speech he had the gift of impressing his hearers deeply. His sermons were dedicated to the service of God, and he was content if they bore good fruit; he did not care what people said about them. He often preached at the evening service for the college servants; but most of all he loved to preach to children, to see the earnest young faces upturned to him, to feel that they were following each word. It was then that he put his whole heart into the task before him; the light grew in his eyes, he forgot to stammer, forgot everything, save the young souls he was leading, in his eagerness to show them the way.

Such was the character of Lewis Carroll up to the year 1862, that momentous year in which he found the golden key of Fairyland. He had often peeped through the closed gates but he had never been able to squeeze through; he might have jumped over them, but that is forbidden in Fairyland, where everything happens in the most natural way.

He had succeeded beyond his hopes in his efforts for independence; he was establishing a brilliant record as a mathematical lecturer; he had several scholarships which paid him a small yearly sum, and he was also sublibrarian. His little poems were making their way into public notice and his more serious work had been "Notes on the First Two Books of Euclid," "Text-Books on Plane Geometry and Plane Trigonometry," and "Notes on the First Part of Algebra."

Socially, the retiring "don" was scarcely known beyond the University. He ran up to London whenever the theaters offered anything tempting; he visited the studios of well-known artists, who were all fond of him, and he cultivated the friendship of men of learning and letters. If these gentlemen happened to have attractive little daughters, he cultivated their acquaintance also. One special anecdote we have of a visit to the studio of Mr. Munroe, where he found two of the children of George Macdonald, the author of many books, among them "At the Back of the North Wind," a most charming fairy tale. These two children, a boy and a girl, instantly made friends with Lewis Carroll, who suggested to the boy, Greville, that he thought a marble head would be such a useful thing, much better than a real one because it would not have to be brushed and combed. This appealed to the small boy, whose long hair was a torment, but after consideration he decided that a marble head would not be able to speak, and it was better to have his hair pulled and be able to cry out. In the case of the general small boy Lewis Carroll preferred marble, but he was overruled. Mr. Macdonald's two daughters, Lily and Mary, were, however, great favorites of his; indeed, his girl friends were rapidly multiplying. Sometimes they came to see him in the pleasant rooms at Christ Church College, which were full of curious things that children love. Sometimes they had tea with him or went for a stroll, for Oxford had many beautiful walks about her colleges.

A visit to him was always a great event, but perhaps those who enjoyed him most were his intimates in "Tom Quadrangle." The three little Liddell girls were at that time his special favorites; their bright companionship brought forth the many sides of his genius; under the spell of their winsome chatter the long golden afternoon would glide happily by, while under *his*spell they would sit for hours listening to the wonder tales he spun for them.

Chapter VI

Up and Down the River with the Real Alice

We generally speak of Oxford-on-the-Thames. Indeed, if we were to journey by water from London to Oxford, we would certainly go by way of the Thames, and a pleasant journey that would be, too, gliding between well-wooded, fertile shores with charming landscape towns on either side and bits of history peeping out in unexpected places. But into the heart of Oxford itself the Thames sends forth its tributaries in opposite directions; the Isis on one side, the Cherwell on the other. The Cherwell is what is called a "canoe river," the Isis is the race course of Oxford, where all the "eights" (every racing crew consists of eight men) come to practice for the great day and the great race, which takes place sometimes at Henley, sometimes at Oxford itself, when the Isis is gay with bunting and flags.

On one side of Christ Church Meadow is a long line of barges which have been made stationary and which are used as boathouses by the various college clubs; these are situated just below what is known as Folly Bridge, a name familiar to all Oxford men, and the goal of many pleasant trips. The original bridge was destroyed in 1779, but tradition tells us that the first bridge was capped by a tower which was the study or observatory of Roger Bacon, the Franciscan Friar who invented the telescope, gunpowder, and many other things unknown to the people of his time. It was even hinted that he had cunningly built this tower that it might fall instantly on anyone passing beneath it who proved to be more learned than himself. One could see it from Christ Church Meadow, and doubtless Lewis Carroll pointed it out to his small companions, as they strolled across to the water's edge, where perhaps a boat rocked lazily at its moorings.

It was the work of a moment to steady it so that the eager youngsters could scramble in, then he stepped in himself, pushing off with his oar, and a few long, steady strokes brought them in midstream. This was an ordinary afternoon occurrence, and the children alone knew the delights of being the chosen companions of Lewis Carroll. He would let them row, while he would lounge among the cushions and "spin yarns" that brought peals of merry laughter that rippled over the surface of the water. He knew by heart every story and tradition of Oxford, from the time the Romans reduced it from a city of some importance to a mere "ford for oxen to pass over," which, indeed, was the origin of its name, long before the Christian era.

He had a story or a legend about every place they passed, but most of all they loved the stories he "made up" as he went along. He had a low, well-pitched voice, with the delightful trick of dropping it in moments of profound interest, sometimes stopping altogether and closing his eyes in pretended sleep, when his listeners were truly thrilled. This, of course, produced a stampede, which he enjoyed immensely, and sometimes he would "wake up," take the oars himself, and pull for some green shady nook that loomed invitingly in the distance; here they would land and under the friendly trees they would have their tea, perhaps, and then they *might* induce him to finish the story—if they were *ever* so good.

It was on just such an occasion that he chanced to find the golden key to Wonderland. The time was midsummer, the place on the way up the river toward Godstow Bridge; the company consisted of three winsome little girls, Lorina, Alice, and Edith Liddell, or *Prima*, *Secunda*, and *Tertia*, as he called them by number in Latin. He tells of this himself in the following dainty poem—the introduction to "Alice in Wonderland":

> All in the golden afternoon
>> Full leisurely we glide;
> For both our oars, with little skill,
>> By little arms are plied,
> While little hands make vain pretence
>> Our wanderings to guide.

Ah, cruel Three! In such an hour,
    Beneath such dreamy weather,
To beg a tale, of breath too weak
    To stir the tiniest feather!
Yet what can one poor voice avail
    Against three tongues together?

Imperious Prima flashes forth
    Her edict "to begin it"—
In gentler tone Secunda hopes
    "There will be nonsense in it"—
While Tertia interrupts the tale,
    Not *more* than once a minute.

Anon, to sudden silence won,
    In fancy they pursue
The dream-child moving through a land
    Of wonders wild and new,
In friendly chat with bird or beast—
    And half believe it true.

And ever as the story drained
    The wells of fancy dry,
And faintly strove that weary one
    To put the subject by,
"The rest next time"—"It *is* next time!"
    The happy voices cry.

Thus grew the tale of Wonderland:
    Thus slowly one by one,
Its quaint events were hammered out—
    And now the tale is done,
And home we steer, a merry crew,
    Beneath the setting sun.

Alice! a childish story take,
    And with a gentle hand

> Lay it where Childhood's dreams are twined
> In Memory's mystic band,
> Like pilgrims' withered wreath of flowers
> Plucked in a far-off land.

It was a very hot day, the fourth of July, 1862, that this special little picnic party set out for its trip up the river. Godstow Bridge was a quaint old-fashioned structure of three arches. In the very middle it was broken by a tiny wooded island, and guarding the east end was a picturesque inn called *The Trout*. Through the middle arch they could catch a distant glimpse of Oxford, with Christ Church spire quite plainly to be seen. They had often gone as far as the bridge and had their tea in the ruins of the old nunnery near by, a spot known to history as the burial-place of Fair Rosamond, that beautiful lady who was supposed to have been poisoned by Queen Eleanor, the jealous wife of Henry II. But this day the sun streamed down on the little party so pitilessly that they landed in a cool, green meadow and took refuge under a hayrick. Lewis Carroll stretched himself out at full length in the protecting shade, while the expectant little girls grouped themselves about him.

"Now begin it," demanded Lorina, who was called *Prima* in the poem. *Secunda* [Alice] probably knew the story-teller pretty well when she asked for nonsense, while tiny *Tertia*, the youngest, simply clamored for "more, more, more," as the speaker's breath gave out.

Now, as Lewis Carroll lay there, a thousand odd fancies elbowing one another in his active brain, his hands groping in the soft moist earth about him, his fingers suddenly closed over that magic Golden Key. It was a queer invisible key, just the kind that fairies use, and neither Lorina, Alice, nor Edith would have been able to find it if they had hunted ever so long. He must have found it on the water and brought it ashore quite by accident, for there was the gleam of sunlight still upon it, and it was very shady under the hayrick. Perhaps there was a door somewhere that the key might fit; but no, there was only the hayrick towering above him, and only the brown earth stretching all about him. Perhaps a white rabbit *did* whisk by, perhaps the real Alice *really* fell asleep, at any rate when *Prima* said "Begin it," that is how he started. The Golden Key opened the brown earth—in popped the white rabbit—down dropped the sleeping Alice—down—down—down—and while she was falling, clutching at things on the way, Lewis Carroll turned, with one of his rare sweet smiles, to the eager trio and began the story of "Alice's Adventures Underground."

The whole of that long afternoon he held the children spellbound. He did not finish the story during that one sitting. Summer has many long days, and the quiet, prudent young "don" was not reckless enough to scatter *all* his treasures at once; and, besides, all the queer things that happened to Alice would have lost half their interest in the shadow of a hayrick, and how could one conjure up *Mock Turtles* and *Lorys* and *Gryphons* on the dry land? Lewis Carroll's own recollection of the beginning of "Alice" is certainly dated from that "golden afternoon" in the boat, and any idea of publishing the web of nonsense he was weaving never crossed his mind. Indeed, if he could have imagined that his small audience of three would grow to be as many millions in the years to come, the book would have lost half its charm, and the real child that lay hidden under the cap and gown of this grave young Student of thirty might never have been known to the world.

Into his mind, with all the freshness of unbidden thought, popped this story of *Alice* and her strange adventures, and while he chose the name of Alice in seeming carelessness, there is no doubt that the little maid who originally owned the name had many points in common with the Rev. Charles Lutwidge Dodgson, never suspected save by the two most concerned.

To begin with, the real Alice had an Imagination; any child who demands nonsense in a story has an Imagination. Nothing was too impossible or absurd to put into a story, for one could always "make believe" it was something else you see, and a constant "make believe" made everything seem quite real. Dearly as he loved this posy of small girls, Lewis Carroll could not help being just the *least* bit partial to Alice, because, as he himself might have quaintly expressed it, she understood everything he said, even before he said it.

She was a dear little round, chubby child, a great camera favorite and consequently a frequent visitor to his rooms, for he took her picture on all occasions. One, as a beggar child, has become quite famous. She is pictured standing, with her ragged dress slipping from her shoulders and her right hand held as if begging for pennies; the other hand rests upon her hip, and her head is bent in a meek fashion; but the mouth has a roguish curve, and there is just the shadow of a laugh in the dark eyes, for of course it's only "make believe," and no one knows it better than Alice herself. Lewis Carroll liked the little bit of acting she did in this trifling part. A child's acting always appealed to him, and many of his youngest and best friends were regularly on the stage.

He took another picture of the children perched upon a sofa; Lorina in the center, a little sister nestling close to her on either side, making a pretty pyramid of the three dark heads. Yet in studying the faces one can understand why it was Alice who inspired him. Lorina's eyes are looking straight ahead, but the lids are dropped with a little conscious air, as if the business of having one's picture taken was a very serious matter, to say nothing of the responsibility of keeping two small sisters in order. Edith is staring the camera out of countenance, uncertain whether to laugh or to frown, a pretty child with curls drooping over her face; but Alice, with the elf-locks and the straight heavy "bang," is looking far away with those wonderful eyes of hers; perhaps she was even then thinking of Wonderland, perhaps even then a light flashed from her to Lewis Carroll in the shape of a promise to take her there some day. At any rate, if it hadn't been for Alice there would have been no Wonderland, and without Wonderland, childhood is but a tale half-told, and even to this day, nearly fifty years since that "golden afternoon," every little girl bearing the name of Alice who has read the book and has anything of an imagination, firmly believes that *she* is the sole and only Alice who could venture into Lewis Carroll's Wonderland.

After he had told the story and the original Alice had expressed her approval, he promised to write it out for her to keep. Of course this took time, because, in the first place, his writing was not quite plain enough for a child to read easily, so every letter was carefully printed. Then the illustrations were troublesome, and he drew as many as he could, consulting a book on natural history for the correct forms of the queer animals *Alice* found. The *Mock Turtle* was his own invention, for there never *was* such an animal on land or sea.

This book was handed over to the small Alice, who little dreamed at that time of the treasure she was to have in her keeping. Over twenty years later, when Alice had become Mrs. Reginald Hargreaves, the great popularity of "Alice in Wonderland" tempted the publishers to bring out a reproduction of the original manuscript. This could not be done without borrowing the precious volume from the original Alice, who was willing to trust it in the hands of her old friend, knowing how over-careful he would be, and, as he resolved that he would not allow any workman to touch it, he had some funny experiences.

To reproduce a book it must first be photographed, and of course Lewis Carroll consulted an expert. He offered to bring the book to London, to go daily to his studio and hold it in position to be photographed, turning over the pages one by one, but the photographer wished to do all that himself. Finally, a man was found who was willing to come to Oxford and do the work in Lewis Carroll's own way, while he stood near by turning over the pages himself rather than let him touch them.

The photographer succeeded in getting a fine set of negatives, and in October, 1880, Lewis Carroll sent the book in safe custody back to its owner, thinking his troubles were over. The next step was to have plates made from the pictures, and these plates in turn could pass into print. The photographer was prompt at first in delivering the plates as they were made, but, finally, like the *Baker* in "The Hunting of the Snark," he "softly and suddenly vanished away," holding still twenty-two of the fine blocks on which the plates were made, leaving the book so far—incomplete.

There ensued a lively search for the missing photographer. This lasted for months, thereby delaying the publication of the book, which was due Christmas. Then, as suddenly as he had disappeared, he reappeared like a ghost at the publishers, left eight of the twenty-two zinc blocks, and again vanished. Finally, when a year had passed and poor Lewis Carroll, at his wits' end, had resolved to borrow the book again in order to photograph the remaining fourteen pages, the man was frightened by threats of arrest, and delivered up the fourteen negatives which he had not yet transferred to the blocks.

The distracted author was glad to find them, even though he had to pay a second time for getting the blocks done properly. However, the book was finished in time for the Christmas sale of 1886, just twenty-one years after "Alice" made her first bow, and the best thing about it was that all the profits were given to the Children's Hospitals and Convalescent Homes for Sick Children. It was thoroughly illustrated with thirty-seven of the author's own drawings, and the grown-up "Alice" received a beautiful special copy bound in white vellum; but pretty as it was, it could not take the place of that other volume carefully written out for the sole pleasure of one little girl. Nothing was too much trouble if it succeeded in giving pleasure to any little girl whom Lewis Carroll knew and loved; even those he did not really know, and consequently could not love, he sought to please, just because they were "little girls."

Alice was among the chosen few who retained his friendship through the years. She was his first favorite, and she was indirectly the source of his good luck, and we may be sure there was a certain winsomeness about her long after the elf-locks were gathered into decorous coils of dark hair.

True, the formal old bachelor came forward in their later association, and the numerous letters he wrote her always began "My dear Mrs. Hargreaves," but his fondness for her outlived many other passing affections.

To go back to the little Alice and the fair smiling river, and that wizard Lewis Carroll, who told the wonder tales so long ago. Once the children had a taste of "Alice," she grew to be a great favorite; sometimes a chapter was told on the river, sometimes in his study, often in the garden or after tea in Christ Church Meadows—in fact, wherever they caught a glimpse of the grave young man in cap and gown, the trio of small Liddells fell upon him, and in this fashion, as he tells us himself, "the quaint events were hammered out."

When he presented the promised copy it might have passed forever from his mind, which was full of the higher mathematics he was teaching to the young men of Christ Church, but he chanced one day to show the manuscript to George Macdonald, the well-known writer, who was so charmed with it that he advised his friend to send it to a publisher. He accordingly carried it to London, and Macmillan & Co. took it at once. This was a great surprise. He never dreamed of his nonsense being considered seriously, and growing suddenly about as young as a great, big, bashful boy, he refused to allow his own rough illustrations to appear in print, so he hunted over the long list of his artist friends, for the genius who could best illustrate the adventures of his dream-child. At last his friend, Tom Taylor, a well-known dramatist, suggested Mr. Tenniel, the clever cartoonist for *Punch*, who was quite willing to undertake this rather odd bit of work, and on July 4, 1865, exactly three years since that memorable afternoon, Alice Liddell received the first printed copy of "Alice in Wonderland," the name the author finally selected for his book.

His first idea, as we know, was "Alice's Adventures Underground," the second was "Alice's Hour in Elfland," but the last seemed best of all, for Wonderland might mean any place where wonderful things could happen. And this was Lewis Carroll's idea; anywhere the dream "Alice" chose to go would be Wonderland, and none knew better than he did how eagerly the child-mind paints its own fairy nooks and corners.

He was not at all excited about his first big venture; no doubt Alice herself took much more interest. To feel that you are about to be put into print is certainly a great experience, almost as great as being photographed; and, knowing how conscientious Lewis Carroll was about little things, we may be quite sure that her suggestions crept into many of the pictures, while it is equally certain that the few additions he made to the original "Alice" were carefully considered and firmly insisted upon by this critical young person.

The first edition of two thousand copies was a great disappointment; the pictures were badly printed, and all who had bought them were asked to send them back with their names and addresses, as a new edition would be printed immediately and they would then receive perfect copies. The old copies Lewis Carroll gave away to various homes and hospitals, while the new edition, upon which he feared a great loss, sold so rapidly that he was astonished, and still more so when edition after edition was demanded by the public, and far from being a failure, "Alice in Wonderland" brought her author both fame and money.

From that time forward, fortune smiled upon him; there were no strenuous efforts to increase his income. "Alice" yielded him an abundance each year, and he was beset by none of the cares and perplexities which are the dragons most writers encounter with their literary swords. He welcomed the fortune, not so much for the good it brought to him alone, but for the power it gave him to help others. His countless charities are not recorded because they were swallowed up in the "little things" he did, not in the great benefits which are trumpeted over the world. His own life, so simple, so full of purpose, flowed on as usual; he was not one to change his habits with the turn of Fortune's wheel, no matter what it brought him.

Of course, everyone knew that a certain Lewis Carroll had written a clever, charming book of nonsense, called "Alice in Wonderland"; that he was an Oxford man, very much of a scholar, and little known outside of the University. What people did not know was that this same Lewis Carroll had for a double a certain "grave and reverend" young "don," named Charles Lutwidge Dodgson, who, while "Alice" was making the whole world laugh, retired to his sanctum and wrote in rapid succession the following learned pamphlets: "The Condensation of Determinants," "An Elementary Treatise on Determinants," "The Fifth Book of Euclid, treated Algebraically," "The Algebraic Formulæ for Responsions."

Now, whatever these may be, they certainly did not interest children in the least, and Charles Lutwidge Dodgson did not care in the least, so long as he could smooth the thorny path of mathematics for his struggling undergraduates. But Lewis Carroll was quite a different matter. So long as the children were pleased, little he cared for algebra or geometry.

A funny tale is told about Queen Victoria. It seems that Lewis Carroll sent the second presentation copy of "Alice in Wonderland" to Princess Beatrice, the Queen's youngest daughter. Her mother was so pleased with the book that she asked to have the author's other works sent to her, and we can imagine her surprise when she received a large package of learned treatises by the mathematical lecturer of Christ Church College.

Who can tell through what curious byways the thought of the dream-child came dancing across the flagstones of the great "Tom Quad." Yet across those same flagstones danced the little Liddells when they thought there was any possibility of a romp or a story; for Lewis Carroll lived in the northwest angle, while the girls lived in the beautiful deanery in the northeast angle, and it was only a "puss-in-the-corner" game to get from one place to the other.

"Alice" was written on the ground floor of this northwest angle, and it was in this sunny room that Lewis Carroll and the real Alice held many a consultation about the new book.

All true fame is to a certain extent due to accident; an act of heroism is generally performed on the spur of the moment; a great poem is an inspiration; a great invention, though preceded possibly by years of study, is born of a single moment's inspiration; so "Alice" came to Lewis Carroll on the wings of inspiration. His study of girls and their varying moods has left its impress on a world of little girls, and there is scarcely a home to-day, in England or America, where there is not a special niche reserved for "Alice in Wonderland," while this interesting young lady has been served up in French, German, Italian, and Dutch, and the famous poem of *Father William* has even been translated into Arabic. Whether the Chinese or the Japanese have discovered this funny little dream-child we cannot tell, but perhaps in time she may journey there and amuse the little maids with the jet-black hair, the creamy skin, and the slanting eyes. Perhaps she may even stir them to laughter.

Surely all must agree that the *Gryphon* himself bears a strong resemblance to the Chinese dragons, and it *might* be, such are the wonders of Wonderland, that the *Mock Turtle* can be found in Japan. Who knows! At any rate the little English Alice never thought of the consequences of that "golden afternoon"; it was good to be in the boat, to pull through the rippling waters and stir a faint breeze as the oars

> "with little skill—
> By little arms are plied";

then to gather under the friendly shade of the hayrick and listen to the wonder tale "with lots of nonsense in it."

Dear little Alice of Long Ago! To you we owe a debt of gratitude. All the little Alices of the past and all the little Alices of the future will have their Wonderland because, while floating up and down the river with the real Alice, Lewis Carroll found the Golden Key.

Chapter VII

Alice in Wonderland and What She did there

A certain little girl who had been poring over "Through the Looking-Glass and What Alice Found There" with eager interest, when asked which of the "Alices" she preferred, answered at once that she thought "Through the Looking-Glass" was "stupider" than "Alice in Wonderland," and when people laughed she was surprised, for she had enjoyed both books.

Stupid was certainly not the word she meant to use, nor yet *silly*, which might have suggested itself if she had stopped to think. *Nonsense* is really what she meant, and only very poor nonsense can be stupid or silly. Good nonsense is exceedingly clever; it takes clever people to write it and only clever people can understand and appreciate it, so when the real Alice hoped "there would be nonsense in it" she was only looking for what she was sure to find: something odd, bright, and funny, with a laugh tucked away in unexpected places.

Nonsense is very ancient and respectable, tracing its origin back to the days of the Court Fool, whose office it was to make merry for the king and courtiers. An undersized man was usually selected, one with some deformity being preferred, whereat the courtiers might laugh; one with sharp tongue and ready wit, to make the time fly. He was clothed in "motley"—that is, his dress, cut in the fashion of the times, was of many ill-assorted hues, while the fool's cap with its bells, and the bauble or rattle which he held in his hand, completed his grotesque appearance.

To the Fool was allowed the freedom of the court and a close intimacy with his royal master, to whom he could say what he pleased without fear of offense; his duty was to amuse, and the sharper his wit the better. It was called nonsense, though a sword could not thrust with keener malice, and historic moments have often hung upon a fool's jest. The history of the Court Fool is the history of mediæval England, France, Spain, and Italy, of a time when a quick figure of speech might turn the tide of war, and the Fool could reel off his "nonsense" when others dared not speak. No one was spared; the king himself was often the victim of the fool's tongue, and under the guise of nonsense much wisdom lurked.

So it has been ever since; the Court Jester has passed away with other old court customs, but the nonsense that was "writ in books" lived after them, so good, so wholesome that we laugh at it with its old-time swing and sting.

The nonsense that we find in books to-day is of a higher order than that of the poor little Court Fool who, swaggering outwardly, trembled inwardly, as he sent his barbed shaft of wit against some lordly breast. The wisdom hides in the simple fun of everyday that makes life a thing of sunshine and holds the shadows back.

Lewis Carroll had this gift of nonsense more than any other writer of his time. Dickens and Thackeray possessed wit and humor of a high quality, but they could not command so large an audience, for children turn to healthy nonsense as sunflowers to the sun, and Lewis Carroll gave them all they wanted. "Grown-ups," too, began to listen, detecting behind the fun much, perhaps, which had escaped even the author himself, until he put on his "grown-up" glasses and began to ponder.

Where the real charm lies in "Alice in Wonderland" would be very difficult to say. If a thousand children were asked to pick out their favorite parts, it is probable that not ten of them would think alike. A great many would say "I like *any* part," and really with such a fascinating book how can one choose? The very opening is enough to cure any little girl of drowsiness on a summer day, and the picture of the pompous little *White Rabbit* with his bulging waistcoat and his imposing watch chain, for all the world like an everyday Englishman, is a type no doubt that the lively little girls and the grave young "don" knew pretty well.

Every page gives one something to think about. To begin with, the fact that *Alice* is dreaming, is plain from the beginning, and that very odd sensation of falling through space often comes during the first few moments of sleep. A busy dreamer can accomplish a great deal in a very short time, as we all know, and the most remarkable things happen in the simplest way. There is a story, for instance, of one little girl, who, after a nice warm bath, was carried to bed and tucked in up to her rosy chin. Her heavy eyes shut immediately and lo! in half a minute she was back in the big porcelain tub, splashing about like a little mermaid; then nurse pulled the stopper out, and through the waste-pipe went water, small girl, and all. When she opened her eyes with a start, she found she had been dreaming *not quite two minutes*. So suppose the real Alice had been dreaming a half an hour; it was quite long enough to skip through "Wonderland," and to have delightful and curious things constantly happening.

It was the *White Rabbit* talking to himself that first attracted her, but a short stay in "Wonderland" got her quite used to all sorts of animals and their funny talk, and the way *she* had of growing larger or smaller on the shortest notice was very puzzling and amusing. How like real people was this dream-child; how many everyday folks find themselves too small for great places, and too great for the small ones, and how many experiments they try to make themselves larger or smaller! You see Lewis Carroll thought of all this, though he did not spoil his story by stopping to explain. It is, indeed, poor nonsense that has to be explained every step of the way.

The dream "Alice" just at first was apt to cry if anything unusual or unpleasant happened; a bad habit with some children, the *real* Alice was given to understand. At any rate, when she drank out of the bottle that tasted of "cherry tart, custard, pineapple, roast turkey, toffy, and hot buttered toast," and found herself growing smaller and smaller, she cried, because she was only ten inches high and could not possibly reach the Golden Key on the glass table. Then she took herself to task very sharply, saying: "Come, there's no use in crying like that! I advise you to leave off this minute!"

"She generally gave herself very good advice (though she seldom followed it), and sometimes she scolded herself so severely as to bring tears into her eyes, and once she remembered trying to box her own ears for having cheated herself in a game of croquet she was playing against herself, for this curious child was very fond of pretending to be two people. 'But it's no use now,' thought poor Alice, 'to pretend to be two people, when there's hardly enough left of me to make *one* respectable person.'"

Then when she found the little glass box with a cake in it marked *"Eat Me"* in currants, she decided that if she ate it something different might happen, for otherwise she would go out like a candle if she grew any smaller. Of course, as soon as she swallowed the whole cake, she took a start and soon stood nine feet high in her slippers.

"'Curiouser and curiouser!' cried Alice (she was so surprised that for the moment she quite forgot to speak good English), 'now I'm opening out like the largest telescope that ever was. Good-bye, feet!' (for when she looked down at her feet they seemed to be almost out of sight, they were getting so far off.) 'Oh, my poor little feet! I wonder who will put on your shoes and stockings for you now, dears? I'm sure *I* shan't be able! I shall be a great deal too far off to trouble myself about you; you must manage the best way you can; but I must be kind to them,' thought Alice, 'or perhaps they won't walk the way I want to go! Let me see: I'll give them a new pair of boots every Christmas.'"

"And she went on planning to herself how she would manage it. 'They must go by the carrier,' she thought; 'and how funny it'll seem, sending presents to one's own feet, and how odd the directions will look!

Alice's Right Foot, Esq.,
Hearthrug,
near the Fender,
(with Alice's love).

Oh, dear, what nonsense I'm talking.'"

Perhaps it was just here that the children's merriment broke forth; the idea of *Alice* being nine feet high was *too* ridiculous, but the poor dream "Alice" didn't think so, for she sat down and began to cry again.

"'You ought to be ashamed of yourself,' said Alice, 'a great girl like you' (she might well say this) 'to go on crying in this way! Stop this moment I tell you!' But she went on all the same, shedding gallons of tears until there was a large pool all around her about four inches deep and reaching half down the hall."

This change she found more puzzling still: everything seemed mixed up, the Multiplication Table, Geography, even the verses which had been familiar to her from babyhood. She tried to say *"How doth the little busy bee,"* but the words would not come right; instead she began repeating, in a hoarse, strange voice, the following noble lines:

> "How doth the little crocodile
> Improve his shining tail,
> And pour the waters of the Nile
> On every golden scale!

> "How cheerfully he seems to grin,
> How neatly spreads his claws,
> And welcomes little fishes in,
> With gently smiling jaws!"

Naturally this produced a sensation, for where is the child who speaks English who does not know that the busy bee "improves the shining hours!"

When the book was translated into French, however, this odd little rhyme not being known to the French children, the translator, M. Henri Bué, had to substitute something else which they could understand—one of their own French rhymes made into a parody of La Fontaine's "Maître Corbeau" (Master Raven).

When *Alice* began to shrink again, she went suddenly *splash* into that immense pool of tears she had shed when she was nine feet high. *Now* she was only two feet high and the water was up to her chin. It was so salty, being tear-water, that she thought she had fallen into the sea, and in this sly fashion Lewis Carroll managed to smuggle in a timely word about the sad way some little girls have of shedding "oceans of tears" on the most trifling occasion.

It was on this briny trip that she fell in with the numbers of queer animals who had also taken refuge in the "Pool of Tears," from the *Mouse* to the *Lory*, who had all fallen into the water and were eagerly swimming toward the shore. They gained it at last and sat there, "the birds with draggled feathers, the animals with their fur clinging close to them, and all dripping wet, cross, and uncomfortable," including *Alice* herself, whose long hair hung wet and straggling on her shoulders.

The *Lory*, of all the odd animals, was probably the oddest. *Alice* found herself talking familiarly with them all, and entering into quite a lengthy argument with the *Lory* in particular about how to get dry. But the *Lory* "turned sulky and would only say: 'I am older than you and must know better,' and this 'Alice' would not allow without knowing how old it was, and as the 'Lory' positively refused to tell its age, there was nothing more to be said."

Lewis Carroll himself made some interesting notes on the life history of this remarkable animal, which were first produced in *The Rectory Umbrella* long before he thought of popping it into "Wonderland." "This creature," he writes, "is, we believe, a species of parrot. Southey informs us that it is a bird of gorgeous plumery [plumage], and it is our private opinion that there never existed more than one, whose history, as far as practicable, we will now lay before our readers."

"The time and place of the Lory's birth is uncertain; the egg from which it was hatched was most probably, to judge from the color of the bird, one of those magnificent Easter eggs which our readers have doubtless seen. The experiment of hatching an Easter egg is at any rate worth trying."

After a lengthy and confusing description he winds up as follows:

"Having thus stated all we know and a great deal we don't know on this interesting subject, we must conclude."

Alice looked upon this domineering old bird of uncertain age quite as a matter of course, as, indeed, she looked upon everything that happened in Wonderland.

There is fun bubbling over in every situation. Sir John Tenniel has given us a clever picture of the wet, woe-begone animals, all clustering around the *Mouse*, who had undertaken to make them dry. "Ahem!" said the Mouse, with an important air, "are you all ready? This is the driest thing I know," and off he rambled into some dull corner of English history, most probably taken out of *Alice's* own lesson book, not unknown to Lewis Carroll.

The Caucas race was suggested by the *Dodo* as an excellent method for getting dry, and as it was a race in which everyone came in ahead, everyone of course was satisfied, and in the distribution of prizes no one was forgotten. *Alice* herself received her own thimble, which she fished out of her pocket, and which the *Dodo* solemnly handed back to her, "saying: 'We beg your acceptance of this elegant thimble,' and when it had finished this short speech they all cheered."

Dinah, the real Alice's real cat, plays an important part in the drama of Wonderland, although she was left at home dozing in the sun; *Alice* mortally offended the *Mouse*, and frightened many of her bird friends almost to death, simply by bringing her into the conversation.

It is certainly delightful to follow in the footsteps of this dream-child of Lewis Carroll's; we lose ourselves in the mazes of Wonderland, and even as we grow older we do not feel that we have to stoop in the least to pass through the portals.

There was a certain air of sociability in Wonderland that pleased *Alice* immensely, for her visiting-list was quite astonishing, and she was continually meeting new—well, not exactly people, but experiences. Her talk with a caterpillar during one of those periods when she was barely tall enough to peep over the mushroom on which he was sitting is "highly amusing and instructive."

"'Who are you?' said the Caterpillar.

"This was not an encouraging opening for a conversation. Alice replied rather shyly: 'I—I hardly know, sir, just at present: at least I know who I was when I got up this morning, but I think I must have changed several times since then.'

"'What do you mean by that?' said the Caterpillar sternly. 'Explain yourself!'

"'I can't explain *myself*, I'm afraid, sir,' said Alice, 'because I'm not myself, you see.'

"'I don't see,' said the Caterpillar.

"'I'm afraid I can't put it more clearly,' Alice replied, very politely, 'for I can't understand it myself to begin with, and being so many different sizes in a day is very confusing.'

"'It isn't,' said the Caterpillar.

"'Well, perhaps you haven't found it so yet,' said Alice, 'but when you have to turn into a chrysalis—you will some day, you know—and then after that into a butterfly, I should think you'll feel it a little queer, won't you?'

"'Not a bit,' said the Caterpillar.

"'Well, perhaps your feelings may be different,' said Alice; 'all I know is, it would feel very queer to *me*.'

"'You!' said the Caterpillar, contemptuously, 'Who are *you*?' Which brought them back again to the beginning of the conversation."

It was the *Caterpillar* who asked her to recite "You are old, Father William," and *Alice* began in this fashion:

"You are old, Father William," the young man said,
   "And your hair has become very white;
And yet you incessantly stand on your head—
   Do you think at your age it is right?"

"In my youth," Father William replied to his son,
   "I feared it might injure the brain;

But now that I'm perfectly sure I have none,
　　Why, I do it again and again."

"You are old," said the youth, "as I mentioned before,
　　And have grown most uncommonly fat;
Yet you turned a back somersault in at the door—
　　Pray, what is the reason of that?"

"In my youth," said the sage, as he shook his gray locks,
　　"I kept all my limbs very supple
By the use of this ointment—one shilling the box—
　　Allow me to sell you a couple."

"You are old," said the youth, "and your jaws are too weak
　　For anything tougher than suet;
Yet you finished the goose, with the bones and the beak—
　　Pray, how did you manage to do it?"

"In my youth," said his father, "I took to the law,
　　And argued each case with my wife;
And the muscular strength which it gave to my jaw
　　Has lasted the rest of my life."

"You are old," said the youth; "one would hardly suppose
　　That your eye was as steady as ever;
Yet you balanced an eel on the end of your nose—
　　What made you so awfully clever?"

"I have answered three questions, and that is enough,"
　　Said his father; "don't give yourself airs!
Do you think I can listen all day to such stuff?
　　Be off, or I'll kick you downstairs!"

Now *Alice* knew well enough that she had given an awful twist to a pretty and old-fashioned piece of poetry, but for the life of her the old words refused to come. It seemed that with her power to grow large or small on short notice, her memory performed queer antics; she was never sure of it for two minutes together.

One odd thing about her change of size was that she never grew up or dwindled away unless she ate something or drank something. Now every little girl has had similar experience when it came to eating and drinking. "Eat so and so," says a "grown-up," "and you will be tall and strong," and "if you *don't* eat this thing or that, you will be little all your life," so *Alice* was only going through the same trials in Wonderland.

Her meeting with the *Duchess* and the peppery *Cook*, and the screaming *Baby*, and the grinning *Cheshire Cat*, occupied some thrilling moments. She found the *Duchess* conversational but cross, and the *Cook* sprinkling pepper lavishly into *the* soup she was stirring, and *out* of it for the matter of that, so that everybody was sneezing. The *Cat* was the sole exception; it sat on the hearth and grinned from ear to ear. *Alice* opened the conversation by asking the *Duchess*, who was holding the *Baby* and jumping it up and down so roughly that it howled dismally, why the *Cat* grinned in that absurd way.

"'It's a Cheshire Cat,' said the Duchess, and that's why. 'Pig!' She said the last word with such sudden violence that Alice quite jumped; but she saw in another moment that it was addressed to the Baby and not to her, so she took courage and went on again:

"'I didn't know that Cheshire Cats always grinned—in fact I didn't know that Cats *could* grin.'

"'They all can,' said the Duchess, 'and most of 'em do.'

"'I don't know of any that do,' said Alice, very politely, feeling quite pleased to have got into a conversation.

"'You don't know much,' said the Duchess; 'and that's a fact.'

"Alice did not like the tone of this remark and thought it would be well to introduce some other subject of conversation."

Then the *Cook* began throwing things about, and the *Duchess*, to quiet the howling *Baby*, sang the following beautiful lullaby, which she emphasized by a violent shake at the end of every line. Considering Lewis Carroll's rather strong feeling on the boy question, they were most appropriate lines, indeed.

> Speak roughly to your little boy,
>   And beat him when he sneezes;
> He only does it to annoy,
>   Because he know it teases.
>
>   *Chorus.*
> (In which the Cook and the Baby joined.)
>   Wow! wow! wow!
>
> I speak severely to my boy,
>   I beat him when he sneezes,
> For he can thoroughly enjoy
>   The pepper when he pleases!
>
>   *Chorus.*
>   Wow! wow! wow!

Imagine the quiet "don" beating time to this beautiful measure, his blue eyes gleaming with fun, his expressive voice shaded to just the right tones to give color to the chorus, while the little girls chimed in at the proper moment. It was no trouble for him to make rhymes, being endowed with this wonderful gift of nonsense, and in conversation he was equally clever. He gave the *Duchess* quite the air of a learned lady, even though she did not know that mustard was a vegetable. When *Alice* suggested that it was a mineral, she was quite ready to agree. "'There's a large mustard mine near here,' she observed, 'and the moral of that is' [the Duchess had a moral for everything], 'The more there is of mine—the less there is of yours.' 'Oh, I know!' exclaimed Alice, who had not attended to this last remark, 'it's a vegetable. It doesn't look like one but it is.'

"'I quite agree with you,' said the Duchess, 'and the moral of that is, "Be what you would seem to be," or if you'd like to put it more simply, "Never imagine yourself not to be otherwise than what it might appear to others that what you were or might have been was not otherwise than what you had been would have appeared to them to be otherwise."'"

"'I think I should understand that better,' said Alice, very politely, 'if I had it written down, but I can't quite follow it as you say it.'

"'That's nothing to what I could say if I chose,'" the Duchess replied in a pleasant tone.

Alice's talk with the *Cheshire Cat*, which had the remarkable power of appearing and vanishing in portions, the table gossip at the Mad Tea Party, to which she was an uninvited guest, are too well-known to quote. Many a time the Mad Tea Party has been the theme of some nursery play or school entertainment. The *Mad Hatter* and the *March Hare* were certainly the maddest things that ever were. When the *Hatter* complained of his watch being two days wrong, he turned angrily to the *March Hare*, saying:

"'I told you butter wouldn't suit the works.'

"'It was the *best* butter,' the March Hare meekly replied.

"'Yes, but some crumbs must have got in as well,' the Hatter grumbled; 'you shouldn't have put it in with the bread knife.'

"The March Hare took the watch and looked at it gloomily; then he dipped it into his cup of tea and looked at it again; but he could think of nothing better to say than his first remark, 'It was the *best* butter you know.'"

Surely nothing could be more amusing that this party of mad ones, and the sleepy *Dormouse*, who sat between the *March Hare* and the *Hatter*, contributed his share to the fun, while the *Hatter's* songs, which he sang at the concert given by the *Queen of Hearts*, was certainly very familiar to *Alice*. It began:

Twinkle, twinkle, little bat—
How I wonder what you're at!
Up above the world you fly,
Like a tea tray in the sky.
Twinkle, twinkle.

Who but Lewis Carroll could invent such a scene? Who could better plan the little sparkling sentences which gave the nonsense just the glitter which children found so fascinating and so laughable. Yet what did they laugh at after all? What do we laugh at even to-day in glancing over the familiar pages? What is it in the mysterious depths of childhood which Lewis Carroll has caught in his golden web? Perhaps, it is not all mere childhood; we are ourselves but "children of a larger growth," and deep down within us at some time or other fancy runs riot and imagination does the rest. So it was with Lewis Carroll, only *his* fancy soared into genius, carrying with it, as someone has said, "a suggestion of clear and yet soft laughing sunshine. He never made us laugh *at* anything, but always *with* him and his knights and queens and heroes of the nursery rhymes."

Behind much of the world's laughter tears may be hiding, but not so in the case of Lewis Carroll; all is pure mirth that flows from him to us, and above all he possesses that indescribable thing called charm. It lurks in the quaint conversations, in the fluent measure of the songs, in the fantastic scenes so full of ideas that seem to vanish before we quite grasp them—like the *Cheshire Cat*—leaving only the smile behind.

To those of us—the world in short—who were denied the privilege of hearing Lewis Carroll tell his own story, the Tenniel pictures bring Wonderland very close. Our natural history alone would not help us in the least when it came to classifying the many strange animals *Alice* met on her journey. The *Mock Turtle*, the *Gryphon*, the *Lory*, the *Dodo*, the *Cheshire Cat*, the *Fish*and *Frog* footmen—how could we imagine them without the Tenniel "guidebook"? The numberless transformations of *Alice* could hardly be understood without photographs of her in the various stages. And certainly at the croquet party, given by the *Queen of Hearts*, how could anyone imagine a game played with bent-over soldiers for wickets, hedgehogs for croquet balls, and flamingoes for mallets, unless there were accompanying illustrations?

One specially interesting picture shows the *Gryphon* in the foreground; he and *Alice* paid a visit to the *Mock Turtle*, who, by way of entertaining his guests, gave the following description of the Lobster Quadrille. With tears running down his cheeks he began:

"'You have never lived much under the sea' ('I haven't,' said Alice) 'and perhaps you were never introduced to a lobster—' (Alice began to say 'I once tasted—' but she checked herself hastily, and said, 'No, never'), 'so you can have no idea what a delightful thing a Lobster Quadrille is!'

"'No, indeed,' said Alice. 'What sort of a dance is it?'

"'Why,' said the Gryphon, 'you first form into a line along the seashore.'

"'Two lines!' cried the Mock Turtle. 'Seals, turtles, salmon, and so on; then when you've cleared all the jellyfish out of the way—'

"'*That* generally takes some time,' interrupted the Gryphon.

"'You advance twice.'

"'Each with a lobster as a partner!' cried the Gryphon.

"'Of course,' the Mock Turtle said; 'advance twice, set to partners—'

"'Change lobsters and retire in same order,' continued the Gryphon.

"'Then, you know,' the Mock Turtle went on, 'you throw the—'

"'The lobsters!' shouted the Gryphon with a bound into the air.

"'As far out to sea as you can—'

"'Swim after them!' screamed the Gryphon.

"'Turn a somersault in the sea!' cried the Mock Turtle, capering wildly about.

"'Change lobsters again!' yelled the Gryphon at the top of its voice.

"'Back to land again, and—that's all the first figure,' said the Mock Turtle, suddenly dropping his voice, and the two creatures who had been jumping about like mad things all this time sat down again, very sadly and quietly, and looked at Alice."

Who could read this without laughing, with no reason for the laugh but sheer delight and sympathy with the story-teller, and with dancing and motion and all the rest of it. If anyone begins to hunt for the reasons why we like "Alice in Wonderland" that person is either very, very sleepy, or she has left her youth so far behind her that, like the *Lory*, she absolutely refuses to tell her age, in which case she must be as old as the hills.

Then the dance, which the two gravely performed for the little girl, and who can forget the song of the *Mock Turtle*?

"Will you walk a little faster!" said a whiting to a snail,

"There's a porpoise close behind us, and he's treading on my tail.

See how eagerly the lobsters and the turtles all advance!

They are waiting on the shingle—will you come and join the dance?

Will you, won't you, will you, won't you, will you join the dance?

Will you, won't you, will you, won't you, won't you join the dance?

"You can really have no notion how delightful it will be

When they take us up and throw us, with the lobsters, out to sea!"

But the snail replied, "Too far, too far!" and gave a look askance—

Said he thanked the whiting kindly, but he would not join the dance.

Would not, could not, would not, could not, would not join the dance.

Would not, could not, would not, could not, could not join the dance.

"What matters it how far we go?" his scaly friend replied,

"There is another shore, you know, upon the other side,

The farther off from England the nearer is to France;

Then turn not pale, beloved snail, but come and join the
dance.
Will you, won't you, will you, won't you, will you join the
dance?
Will you, won't you, will you, won't you, won't you join the
dance?"

Then *Alice* tried to repeat "'Tis the voice of the Sluggard," but
she was so full of the Lobster Quadrille that the words came like
this:

> 'Tis the voice of the lobster, I heard him declare,
> "You have baked me too brown, I must sugar my hair."
> As a duck with its eyelids, so he with his nose
> Trims his belt and his buttons, and turns out his toes.

The whole time she was in Wonderland she never by any
chance recited anything correctly, and through all of her wanderings
she never met anything in the shape of a little boy, except the infant
son of the *Duchess*, who after all turned out to be a pig and vanished
in the woods. The "roundabouts" played no parts in "Alice in Wonderland," and yet—to a man—they love it to this day.

When at last *Alice* bade farewell to the *Mock Turtle*, she left
it sobbing of course, and singing with much emotion the following
song, entitled:

TURTLE SOUP

> Beautiful Soup, so rich and green,
> Waiting in a hot tureen!
> Who for such dainties would not stoop?
> Soup of the evening, beautiful Soup!
> Soup of the evening, beautiful Soup!
> > Beau—ootiful Soo—oop!
> > Beau—ootiful Soo—oop!
> Soo—oop of the e—e—evening,
> > Beautiful, beautiful Soup!
> Beautiful Soup! Who cares for fish,

> Game, or any other dish
> Who would not give all else for two
> pennyworth only of beautiful Soup?
> Beau—ootiful Soo—oop!
> Beau—ootiful Soo—oop!
> Soo—oop of the e—e—evening,
> Beautiful, beauti—FUL SOUP!

We might spend a whole chapter over the great trial scene of the *Knave of Hearts*. We all know that the wretched fellow stole some tarts upon a summer's day, and that he was brought in chains before the *King* and *Queen*, to face the charges. What we did not know was that it was the fourth of July, and that *Alice* was one of the witnesses.

This, in a certain way, is the cleverest chapter in the book, for all the characters in Wonderland take part in the proceedings, which are so like, and yet so comically unlike, a real court. We forget, as *Alice* did, that all these royalties are but a pack of cards, and follow all the evidence with the greatest interest, including the piece of paper which the *White Rabbit* had just found and presented to the Court. It contained the following verses:

> They told me you had been to her,
> And mentioned me to him:
> She gave me a good character,
> But said I could not swim.

> He sent them word I had not gone
> (We know it to be true):
> If she should push the matter on,
> What would become of you?

> I gave her one, they gave him two,
> You gave us three or more:
> They all returned from him to you,
> Though they were mine before.

> If I or she should chance to be
>   Involved in this affair,
> He trusts to you to set them free,
>   Exactly as we were.
>
> My notion was that you had been
>   (Before she had this fit)
> An obstacle that came between
>   Him, and ourselves, and it.
>
> Don't let him know she liked them best,
>   For this must ever be
> A secret, kept from all the rest,
>   Between yourself and me.

This truly clear explanation touches the *Queen of Hearts* so closely that the outsider is led to believe that she is indirectly responsible for the theft, that the poor knave is but the tool of her Majesty, whose fondness for tarts led her into temptation. Lewis Carroll had a keen eye for the dramatic climax—the packed court room, the rambling evidence, the mystifying scrap of paper, and *Alice's* defiance of the *King* and *Queen*.

"'Off with her head!' the Queen shouted at the top of her voice. Nobody moved. 'Who cares for you?' said Alice (she had grown to her full size by this time), 'you're nothing but a pack of cards.'

"At this, the whole pack rose up in the air and came flying down upon her; she gave a little scream, half of fright, half of anger, and tried to beat them off and found herself lying on the bank, with her head in the lap of her sister, who was gently brushing away some dead leaves that had fluttered down from the trees on to her face...."

And so Alice woke up, shook back the elf-locks, and laughed as she rubbed her eyes.

"Such a curious dream!" she said, as the wonder of it all came back to her, and she told her sister of the queer things she had seen and heard, and long after she had run away, this big sister sat with closed eyes, dreaming and wondering.

"The long grass rustled at her feet as the White Rabbit hurried by; the frightened Mouse splashed his way through the neighboring pool; she could hear the rattle of the teacups as the March Hare and his friends shared their never-ending meal, and the shrill voice of the Queen ordering off her unfortunate guests to execution. Once more the pig-baby was sneezing on the Duchess's knee, while plates and dishes crashed around it; once more the shriek of the Gryphon, the squeaking of the Lizard's slate pencil, and the choking of the suppressed Guinea Pigs filled the air, mixed up with the distant sob of the miserable Mock Turtle."

Yet when she opened her eyes she knew that Wonderland must go. In reality "the grass would only be rustling in the wind, and the pool rippling to the waving of the reeds, the rattling teacups would change to tinkling sheep bells and the Queen's shrill cries to the voice of the shepherd boy, and the sneeze of the baby, the shriek of the Gryphon, and all the other queer noises would change ... to the confused clamor of the busy farmyard, while the lowing of the cattle in the distance would take the place of the Mock Turtle's heavy sobs."

So *we* have dreamed of Wonderland from that time till now, when Lewis Carroll looks out from the pages of his book and says:

"That's all—for to-night—there may be more to-morrow."

Chapter VIII

Lewis Carroll at Home and Abroad

The popularity of "Alice in Wonderland" was a never-ending source of surprise to the author, who had only to stand quietly by and rake in his profits, as edition after edition was swallowed up by a public incessantly clamoring for more, and Lewis Carroll was not too modest to enjoy the sensation he was creating in the literary world. His success came to him unsought, and was all the more lasting because the seeds of it were planted in love and laughter. Let us see what he says in the preface to "Alice Underground," the forerunner, as we know, of "Alice in Wonderland."

"The 'why' of this book cannot and need not be put into words. Those for whom a child's mind is a sealed book, and who see no divinity in a child's smile, would read such words in vain; while for any one who has ever loved one true child, no words are needed. For he will have known the awe that falls on one in the presence of a spirit, fresh from God's hands, on whom no shadow of sin, and but the outermost fringe of the shadow of sorrow, has yet fallen; he will have felt the bitter contrast between the haunting selfishness that spoils his best deeds and the life that is but an overflowing love—for I think a child's first attitude to the world is a simple love for all living things—and he will have learned that the best work a man can do is when he works for love's sake only, with no thought of name or gain or earthly reward. No deed of ours, I suppose, on this side of the grave is really unselfish, yet if one can put forth all one's powers in a task where nothing of reward is hoped for but a little child's whispered thanks, and the airy touch of a little child's pure lips, one seems to have come somewhere near to this."

In the appendix to the same book he writes regarding laughter:

"I do not believe God means us to divide life into two halves—to wear a grave face on Sunday, and to think it out of place even so much as to mention Him on a week-day.... Surely the children's innocent laughter is as sweet in His ears as the grandest anthem that ever rolled up from 'the dim religious light' of some solemn cathedral; and if I have written anything to add to those stores of innocent and healthy amusement that are laid up in books for the children I love so well, it is surely something I may hope to look back upon without shame or sorrow ... when my turn comes to walk through the valley of shadows."

Such was the man who filled the world with laughter, and wrote "nonsense" books; a man of such deeply religious feeling that a jest that touched upon sacred things, however innocent in itself, was sure to bring down his wrath upon the head of the offender. There is a certain strain of sadness in those quoted words of his, which surely never belonged to those "golden summer days" when he made merry with the three little Liddells. We must remember that twenty-one years had passed between the telling of the story and the reprint of the original manuscript, and Lewis Carroll was just a little graver and considerably older than on that eventful day when the *White Rabbit* looked at his watch as if to say: "Oh—my ears and whiskers! What will the Duchess think!" as he popped down the hole with *Alice* at his heels.

But we are going a little too far ahead. After the writing of "Alice," with the accompanying excitement of seeing his first-born win favor, Lewis Carroll went quietly forward in his daily routine. He had already become quite a famous lecturer, being, indeed, the only mathematical lecturer in Christ Church College, so Charles Lutwidge Dodgson was not completely overshadowed by the glory of Lewis Carroll.

From the beginning he was careful to separate these two sides of his life, and the numbers of letters which soon began to pour in upon the latter were never recognized by the grave, precise "don," whose thoughts flowed in numbers, and so it was all through his life. When anyone wrote to him, addressing him by his real name, and praising him for the "Alice" books, he sent a printed reply which he kept "handy," saying that as C. L. Dodgson was so often approached as the author of books bearing another name, it must be understood that Mr. Dodgson never acknowledged the authorship of a book which did not bear his name. He was most careful in the wording of this printed form, that it should bear no shadow of untruth. It was only his shy way of avoiding the notice of strangers, and it succeeded so well that very few people knew that the Rev. Charles Dodgson and Lewis Carroll were one and the same person. It was also hinted, and very broadly, too, that many of the queer characters *Alice* met on her journey through Wonderland were very dignified and stately figures in the University itself, who posed unconsciously as models. The *Hatter* is an acknowledged portrait, and no doubt there were many other sly caricatures, for Lewis Carroll was a born humorist.

"Alice" has been given to the public in many ways besides translations. There have been lectures, plays, magic lantern slides of Tenniel's wonderful pictures, tableaux; and many scenes find their way, even at this day, in the nursery wall-paper covered over with Gryphons and Mock Turtles and the whole Court of Cards—a most imposing array. It has been truly stated that, with the exception of Shakespeare's plays, no books have been so often quoted as the two "Alices."

After the publication of "Alice in Wonderland," Lewis Carroll contributed short stories to the various periodicals which were eager for his work. As early as 1867, he sent to *Aunt Judy's Magazine* a short story called "Bruno's Revenge," the foundation of "Sylvie and Bruno," which was never published in book form until 1889, twenty-two years after.

The editor of the magazine, Mrs. Gatty, in accepting the story, gave the author some wholesome advice wrapped up in a bundle of praise for the dainty little idyll. She reminded him that mathematical ability such as he possessed was also the gift of hundreds of others, but his story-telling talent, so full of exquisite touches, was peculiarly his own, and whatever of fame might come to him would be on the wings of the fairies, and not from the lecture room.

In "Bruno's Revenge" we have, for the first time in any of his stories, a little boy. It was a sort of unwilling tribute Lewis Carroll paid to the poor despised "roundabouts," and for all the winsome fairy ways and merry little touches, *Bruno* was never *quite* the real thing; at any rate the story was put away to simmer, and as the long years passed, it was added to bit by bit until—but *that* is another story.

Between the publication of "Alice" and the summer vacation of 1867 he wrote several very learned mathematical works that earned him much distinction among the Christ Church undergraduates, who found it hard to believe that Mr. Dodgson and Lewis Carroll were so closely connected. It was during this summer (1867) that he and Dr. Liddon took a short tour on the Continent.

The two men had much in common and were firm friends. Both had the true Oxford spirit, both were churchmen, Dr. Liddon being quite a famous preacher, and both were men of high intelligence with a good supply of humor; consequently the prospect of a trip to Russia together was a very delightful one. Lewis Carroll kept a journal which was such a complete record of his experiences that at one time he thought of publishing it, though it was never done.

He went up to London on July 12th, remarking in his characteristic way that he and the Sultan of Turkey arrived on the same day, *his* entrance being at Paddington station—the Sultan's at Charing Cross, where, he was forced to admit, the crowd was much greater. He met Dr. Liddon at Dover and they crossed to Calais, finding the passage unusually smooth and uneventful, feeling in some way that they had paid their money in vain, for the trip across the channel is generally one of storm and stress.

All such tours have practically the same object—to see and to enjoy—and the young "don" came out of his den for this express purpose. It had been impossible in the busy years since his graduation to take his holidays far away from home, but at the age of thirty-five he felt that he had earned the right, and proceeded to use it in his own way. Their route lay through Germany, stopping at Cologne, Danzig, Berlin and Königsberg, among other places, and he feasted on the beauties which these various cities had to offer him; the architecture and paintings, the pageantry of strange religions, the music in the great cathedrals, and last, but not least, the foreign drama interested him greatly. The German acting was easy enough to follow, as he knew a little of the language; but the Russian tongue was beyond him, and he could only rely upon the gestures and expression.

Their special object in going to Russia was to see the great fair at Nijni-Novgorod. This fair brought all the corners of the earth together; Chinese, Persians, Tartars, native Russians, mingled in the busy, surging life about them, and lent color and variety to every step. The two friends spent their time pleasantly, for the fame of Dr. Liddon's preaching had reached Russia, and the clergy opened their doors to the travelers and took them over many churches and monasteries, which otherwise they might never have seen. They stopped in Moscow, St. Petersburg, Kronstadt, Warsaw, taking in Leipzig, Giessen, Ems, and many smaller places on the homeward road.

They visited a famous monastery while in Moscow, and were even shown the subterranean cells of the hermits. At Kronstadt they had a most amusing experience. They went to call upon a friend, and Dr. Liddon, forgetting his scanty knowledge of the Russian language, rashly handed his overcoat to one of the servants. When they were ready to leave there was a waiting-maid in attendance—but no overcoat. The damsel spoke no English, the gentleman spoke no Russian, so Dr. Liddon asked for his overcoat with what he considered the most appropriate gesture. Intelligence beamed upon the maiden's face; she ran from the room, returning with a clothes brush. No, Dr. Liddon did not want his coat brushed; he tried other gestures, succeeding so beautifully that the girl was convinced that he wanted to take a nap on the sofa, and brought a cushion and a pillow for that purpose. Still no overcoat, and Dr. Liddon was in despair until Lewis Carroll made a sketch of his friend with one coat on, in the act of putting on another, in the hands of an obliging Russian peasant. The drawing was so expressive that the maid understood at once; the mystery was solved—and the coat recovered.

With this gift of drawing a situation, it is remarkable that Lewis Carroll never became an artist. With all his artistic ideas, and with his real knowledge of art, it seems a pity that he could not have gratified his ambition, but after serious consultation with John Ruskin, who as critic and friend examined his work, he decided that his natural gift was not great enough to push, and sensibly resolved not to waste so much precious time. Still, to the end of his life, he drew for amusement's sake and for the pleasure it gave his small friends.

Altogether their tour was a very pleasant one, and their return was through Germany, that most interesting country of hills and valleys and pretty white villages nestling among the trees. What Lewis Carroll specially liked was the way the old castles seemed to spring out of the rock on which they had been built, as if they had grown there without the aid of bricks and mortar. He admired the spirit of the old architects, which guided them to plan buildings naturally suited to their surroundings, and was never tired of the beautiful hills, so densely covered with small trees as to look moss-grown in the distance.

On his return to Oxford, he plunged at once into very active work. The new term was beginning—there were lectures to prepare and courses to plan, and undergraduates to interview, all of which kept him quite busy for a while, though it did not interfere with certain cozy afternoon teas, when he related his summer adventures to his numerous girl friends, and kept them in a gale of laughter over his many queer experiences.

But these same little girls were clamoring for another book, and a hundred thousand others were alike eager for it, to judge by the heavy budgets of mail he received, so he cast about in that original mind of his for a worthy sequel to "Alice in Wonderland." He was willing to write a sequel then, for "Alice" was still fresh and amusing to a host of children, and its luster had been undimmed as yet by countless imitations. To be sure "Alice in Blunderland" had appeared in *Punch*, the well-known English paper of wit and humor, but then *Punch* was *Punch*, and spared nothing which might yield a ripple of laughter.

When it was known that he had finally determined to write the book, a leading magazine offered him two guineas a page (a sum equal to about ten dollars in our money) for the privilege of printing it as a serial. This story as we know was called "Through the Looking-Glass and What Alice Found There," though few people take time to use the full title. It is usually read by youngsters right "on top" of "Alice in Wonderland." They speak of the two books as the "Alices," and some of the best editions are even bound together, so closely are the stories connected.

With Lewis Carroll's aptness for doing things backward, is it any wonder that he pushed Alice through the Looking-Glass? And so full of grace and beauty and absurd situations is the story he has given us, we quite forget that it was written for the public, and not entirely for three little girls "all on a summer's day." No doubt they heard the chapters for they were right there across "Tom Quad" and could be summoned by a whistle, if need be, along with some other little girls who had sprung up within the walls of Christ Church.

At any rate the story turned out far beyond his expectations and he was again fortunate in securing Tenniel as his illustrator. It was no easy task to illustrate for Lewis Carroll, who criticised every stroke, and being quite enough of an artist to know exactly what he wanted, he was never satisfied until he had it. This often tried the patience of those who worked with him, but his own good humor and unfailing courtesy generally won in the end.

In the midst of this pleasant work came the greatest sorrow of his life, the death of his father, Archdeacon Dodgson, on June 21, 1868. Seventeen years had passed since his mother's death, which had left him stunned on the very threshold of his college life; but he was only a boy in spite of his unusual gravity, and his youth somehow fought for him when he battled with his grief. In those intervening years, he and his father had grown very close together. One never took a step without consulting the other. Christ Church and all it meant to one of them was alike dear to the other. The archdeacon took the keenest interest in his son's outside work, and we may be quite sure that "Alice" was as much read and as thoroughly enjoyed by this grave scholar as by any other member of his household. It was the suddenness of his death which left its lasting mark on Lewis Carroll, and the fact that he was summoned too late to see his father alive. It was a terrible shock, and a grief of which he could never *speak*. He wrote some beautiful letters about it, but those who knew him well respected the wall of silence he erected.

In truth, our quiet, self-contained "don" was a man of deep emotions; the quiet, the poise, had come through years of inward struggle, and he maintained it at the cost of being considered a little cold by people who never could know the trouble it had been to smother the fire. He put away his sorrow with other sacred things, and on his return to Oxford went to work in his characteristic way on a pamphlet concerning the Fifth Book of Euclid, written principally to aid the students during examinations, and which was considered an excellent bit of work.

In November, 1868, he moved into new quarters in Christ Church and, as he occupied these rooms for the rest of his life, a little description of them just here would not be out of place.

"Tom Quad," we must not forget, was the Great Quadrangle of Christ Church, where all the masters and heads of the college lived with their families. This was called being *in residence*, and a pretty sight it was to see the great stretch of green, and its well-kept paths gay with the life that poured from the doors and peeped through the windows of this wonderful place; a sunny day brought out all the young ones, and just here Lewis Carroll's closest ties were formed.

The angles of "Tom Quad" were the choice spots for a lodging, and Lewis Carroll lived in the west angle, first on the ground floor, where, as we know, "Alice in Wonderland" was written; then, when he made his final move, it was to the floor above, which was brighter and sunnier, giving him more rooms and more space. This upper floor looked out upon the flat roof of the college, an excellent place for photography, to which he was still devoted, and he asked permission of those in charge to erect a studio there. This was easily obtained, and could the walls tell tales they would hum with the voices of the celebrated "flies" this clever young "spider" lured into his den. For he took beautiful photographs at a time when photography was not the perfect system that it is now, and nothing pleased him better than posing well-known people. All the big lights of Oxford sat before his camera, including Lord Salisbury, who was Chancellor at that time. Artists, sculptors, writers, actors of note had their pleasant hour in Lewis Carroll's studio.

Our "don" was very partial to great people, that is, the truly great, the men and women who truly counted in the world, whether by birth and breeding or by some accomplished deed or high aim. Being a cultured gentleman himself, he had a vast respect for culture in other people—not a bad trait when all is told, and setting very naturally upon an Englishman born of gentle stock, with generations of ladies and gentlemen at his back. One glance into the sensitive, refined face of Charles Dodgson would convince us at once that no friendship he ever formed had anything but the highest aim for him. He might have chosen for his motto—

"Only what thou art in thyself, not what thou hast, determines thy value."

Even among his girl friends, the "little lady," no matter how poor or plain, was his first object; that was a strong enough foundation. The rest was easy.

But here we have been outside in the studio soaring a bit in the sky, when our real destination is that suite of beautiful big rooms where Lewis Carroll lived and wrote and entertained his many friends, for hospitality was one of his greatest pleasures, and his dining-room and dinner parties are well remembered by every child friend he knew, to say nothing of those privileged elders who were sometimes allowed to join them. He was very particular about his dinners and luncheons, taking care to have upon the table only what his young guests could eat.

He had four sitting rooms and quite as many bedrooms, to say nothing of store-rooms, closets and so forth. His study was a great room, full of comfortable sofas and chairs, and stools and tables, and cubby-holes and cupboards, where many wonderfully interesting things were hidden from view, to be brought forth at just the right moment for special entertainment.

Lewis Carroll had English ideas about comfortable surroundings. He loved books, and his shelves were well filled with volumes of his own choosing; a rare and valuable library, where each book was a tried friend.

A man with so many sitting rooms must certainly have had use for them all, and knowing how methodical he was we may feel quite sure that the room where he wrote "Through the Looking-Glass" was not the sanctum where he prepared his lectures and wrote his books on Logic and Higher Mathematics; it *might* have served for an afternoon frolic or a tea party of little girls; *that* would have been in keeping, as probably he received the undergraduates in his sanctum.

As for the other two sitting rooms, "let's pretend," as Alice herself says, that one was dedicated to the writing of poetry, and the other to the invention of games and puzzles; he had quite enough work of all kinds on hand to keep every room thoroughly aired. We shall hear about these rooms again from little girls whose greatest delight it was to visit them. What we want to do now is to picture Lewis Carroll in his new quarters, energetically pushing Alice through the Looking-Glass, while at the same time he was busily writing "Phantasmagoria," a queer ghost poem which attracted much attention. It was published with a great many shorter poems in the early part of 1869, preceding the publication of the new "Alice," on which he was working chapter by chapter with Sir John Tenniel.

It was wonderful how closely the artist followed the queer mazes of Lewis Carroll's thought. He was able to draw the strange animals and stranger situations just as the author wished to have them, but there came a point at which the artist halted and shook his head.

"I don't like the 'Wasp Chapter,'" was the substance of a letter from artist to author, and he could not see his way to illustrating it. Indeed, even with his skill, a wasp in a wig was rather a difficult subject and, as Lewis Carroll wouldn't take off the wig, they were at a standstill. Rather than sacrifice the wig it was determined to cut out the chapter, and as it was really not so good as the other chapters, it was not much loss to the book, which rounded out very easily to just the dozen, full of the cleverest illustrations Tenniel ever drew. It was his last attempt at illustrating: the gift deserted him suddenly and never returned. His original cartoon work was always excellent, but the "Alices" had brought him a peculiar fame which would never have come to him through the columns of *Punch*, and Lewis Carroll, always generous in praising others, was quick to recognize the master hand which followed his thought. There was something in every stroke which appealed to the laughter of children, and the power of producing unthinkable animals amounted almost to inspiration. No doubt there may be illustrators of the present day quite as clever in their line, but Lewis Carroll stood alone in a new world which he created; there were none before him and none followed him, and his Knight of the Brush was faithful and true.

"Through the Looking-Glass" was published in 1871, and at once took its place as another "Alice" classic. There is much to be said about this book—so much, indeed, that it requires a chapter of its own, for many agree in considering it even more of a masterpiece than "Alice in Wonderland," and though more carefully planned out than its predecessor, there is no hint of hard labor in the brilliant nonsense.

Those who have known and loved the man recognize in the "Alices" the best and most attractive part of him. In spite of his persistent stammering, he was a ready and natural talker, and when in the mood he could be as irresistibly funny as any of the characters in his book. His knowledge of English was so great that he could take the most ordinary expression and draw from it a new and unexpected meaning; his habit of "playing upon words" is one of his very funniest traits. When the *Mock Turtle* said in that memorable conversation with *Alice* which we all know by heart: "no wise fish would go anywhere without a porpoise," he meant, of course, without a *purpose*, and having made the joke he refused explanations and seemed offended that *Alice* needed any. Another humorous idea was that the whitings always held their tails in their mouths.

"The reason is," said the Gryphon, "that they *would* go with the lobsters to the dance. So they were thrown out to sea. So they had to fall a long way. So they got their tails fast in their mouths. So they couldn't get them out again. That's all."

This is not the natural position of the whiting, as we all know, but the device of the fishmonger to make his windows attractive, and *Alice* herself came perilously near saying that she had eaten them for dinner cooked in that fashion and sprinkled over with bread crumbs. It was just Lewis Carroll's funny way of viewing things, in much the same fashion that one of his child-friends would look at them. His was a real child's mind, full of wonder depths where all sorts of impossible things existed, two-sided triangles, parallel lines that met in a point, whitings who had their tails in their mouths, and many other delightful contradictions, some of which he gave to the world. Others he stored away for the benefit of the numberless little girls who had permission to rummage in the store-house.

"Alice through the Looking-Glass" made its bow with a flourish of trumpets. All the "Nonsense" world was waiting for it, and for once expectation was not disappointed and the author found himself almost hidden beneath his mantle of glory. People praised him so much that it is quite a wonder his head was not completely turned. Henry Kingsley, the novelist, thought it "perfectly splendid," and indeed many others fully agreed with him.

As for the children—and after all they were his *real* critics— the little girl who thought "Through the Looking-Glass" "stupider" than Wonderland, voiced the popular sentiment. Those who were old enough to read the book themselves soon knew by heart all the fascinating poetry, and if the story had no other merit, "The Jabberwocky" alone would have been enough to recommend it. Of all the queer fancies of a queer mind, this poem was the most remarkable, and even to-day, with all our clever verse-makers and nonsense-rhymers, no one has succeeded in getting out of apparently meaningless words so much real meaning and genuine fun as are to be found in this one little classic.

Many people have tried in vain to trace its origin; one enterprising lady insisted on calling it a translation from the German. Someone else decided there was a Scandinavian flavor about it, so he called it a "Saga." Mr. A. A. Vansittart, of Trinity College, Cambridge, made an excellent Latin translation of it, and hundreds of others have puzzled over the many "wrapped up" meanings in the strange words.

We shall meet the poem later on and discuss its many wonders. At present we must follow Charles Dodgson back into his sanctum where he was eagerly pursuing a new course—the study of anatomy and physiology. He was presented with a skeleton, and laying in the proper supply of books, he set to work in earnest. He bought a little book called "What to do in Emergencies" and perfected himself in what we know to-day as "First Aid to the Injured." He accumulated in this way some very fine medical and surgical books, and had more than one occasion to use his newly acquired knowledge.

Most men labor all their lives to gain fame. Lewis Carroll was a hard worker, but fame came to him without an effort. Along his line of work he took his "vorpal" sword in hand and severed all the knots and twists of the mathematical Jabberwocky. It was when he played that he reached the heights; when he touched the realm of childhood he was all conquering, for he was in truth a child among them, and every child felt the youthfulness in his glance, in the wave of his hand, in the fitting of his mood to theirs, and his entire sympathy in all their small joys sorrows—such great important things in their child-world. He often declared that children were three fourths of his life, and it seems indeed a pity that none of his own could join the band of his ardent admirers.

Here he was, a young man still in spite of his forty years, holding as his highest delight the power he possessed of giving happiness to other people's children. Yet had anyone ventured to voice this regret, he would have replied like many another in his position:

"Children—bless them! Of course I love them. I prefer other people's children. All delight and no bother. One runs a fearful risk with one's own." And he might have added with his whimsical smile, "And supposing they *might* have been boys!"

Chapter IX

More of 'Alice through the Looking-Glass'

Six years had passed since Alice took her trip through Wonderland, and, strange to say, she had not grown very much older, for Time has the trick of standing still in Fairyland, and when Lewis Carroll pushed her through the Looking-Glass she told everyone she met on the other side that she was seven years and six months old, not very much older, you see, than the Alice of Long Ago, with the elf-locks and the dreamy eyes. The real Alice was in truth six years older now, but real people never count in Fairyland, and surely no girl of a dozen years or more would have been able to squeeze through the other side of a Looking-Glass. Still, though so very young, Alice was quite used to travel, and knew better how to deal with all the queer people she met after her experiences in Wonderland.

Mirrors are strange things. *Alice* had often wondered what lay behind the big one over the parlor mantel, and *wondering* with *Alice* meant *doing*, for presto! up she climbed to the mantelshelf. It was easy enough to push through, for she did not have to use the slightest force, and the glass melted at her touch into a sheet of mist and there she was on the other side!

In the interval between the two "Alices," a certain poetic streak had become strongly marked in Lewis Carroll. To him a child's soul was like the mirror behind which little *Alice* peeped out from its "other side," and gave us the reflection of her child-thoughts.

"Only a dream," we may say, but then child-life is dream-life. So much is "make-believe" that "every day" is dipped in its golden light. It was a dainty fancy to hold us spellbound at the mirror, and many a little girl, quite "unbeknownst" to the "grown-ups," has tried her small best to squeeze through the looking-glass just as *Alice* did. In the days of our grandmothers, when the cheval glass swung in a frame, the "make believe" came easier, for one could creep under it or behind it, instead of through it, with much the same result. But nowadays, with looking-glasses built in the walls, how *can* one pretend properly!

If fairies only knew what examples they were to the average small girl and small boy, they would be very careful about the things they did. Fortunately they are old-fashioned fairies, and have not yet learned to ride in automobiles or flying-machines, else there's no telling what might happen.

Alice was always lucky in finding herself in the very best society—nothing more or less than royalty itself. But the Royal Court of Cards was not to be compared with the Royal Court of Chessmen, which she found behind the fireplace when she jumped down on the other side of the mantel. Of course, it was only "pretending" from the beginning; a romp with the kittens toward the close of a short winter's day, a little girl curled up in an armchair beside the fire with the kitten in her lap, while Dinah, the mother cat, sat near by washing little Snowdrop's face, the snow falling softly without, *Alice* was just the least bit drowsy, and so she talked to keep awake.

"Do you hear the snow against the window panes, Kitty? How nice and soft it sounds! Just as if some one was kissing the window all over outside. I wonder if the snow *loves* the trees and fields that it kisses them so gently? And then it covers them up snug you know with a white quilt; and perhaps it says, 'Go to sleep, darlings, till the summer comes again,' and when they wake up in the summer, Kitty, they dress themselves all in green, and dance about whenever the wind blows. 'Oh, that's very pretty!' cried Alice, dropping the ball of worsted to clap her hands. 'I do so *wish* it was true. I'm sure the woods look sleepy in the autumn when the leaves are getting brown.'"

We are sure, too, *Alice* was getting sleepy in the glow of the firelight with the black kitten purring a lullaby on her lap. She had probably been playing with the Chessmen and pretending as usual, so it is small wonder that the heavy eyes closed, and the black kitten grew into the shape of the *Red Queen*—and so the story began.

It was the work of a few minutes to be on speaking terms with the whole Chess Court which *Alice* found assembled. The back of the clock on the mantelshelf looked down upon the scene with the grinning face of an old man, and even the vase wore a smiling visage. There was a good fire burning in this looking-glass grate, but the flames went the other way of course, and down among the ashes, back of the grate, the Chessmen were walking about in pairs.

Sir John Tenniel's picture of the assembled Chessmen is very clever. The *Red King* and the *Red Queen* are in the foreground. The *White Bishop* is taking his ease on a lump of coal, with a smaller lump for a footstool, while the two *Castles* are enjoying a little promenade near by. In the background are the *Red* and *White Knights* and *Bishops* and all the *Pawns*. He has put so much life and expression into the faces of the little Chessmen that we cannot help regarding them as real people, and we cannot blame *Alice* for taking them very much in earnest.

She naturally found difficulty in accustoming herself to Looking-Glass Land, and the first thing she had to learn was how to read Looking-Glass fashion. She happened to pick up a book that she found on a table in the Looking-Glass Room, but when she tried to read it, it seemed to be written in an unknown language. Here is what she saw:

JABBERWOCKY.

'Twas brillig, and the slithy toves
Did gyre and gimble in the wabe:
All mimsy were the borogoves,
And the mome raths outgrabe.

Then a bright thought occurred to her, and holding the book up before a looking-glass, this is what she read in quite clear English, no matter how it looks, for there is certainly no intelligent child who could fail to understand it.

JABBERWOCKY

'Twas brillig, and the slithy toves
Did gyre and gimble in the wabe:
All mimsy were the borogoves,
And the mome raths outgrabe.

> "Beware the Jabberwock, my son!
>   The jaws that bite, the claws that catch!
> Beware the Jubjub bird, and shun
>   The frumious Bandersnatch!"
>
> He took his vorpal sword in hand:
>   Long time the manxome foe he sought—
> So rested he by the Tumtum tree,
>   And stood awhile in thought.
>
> And, as in uffish thought he stood,
>   The Jabberwock, with eyes of flame,
> Came whiffling through the tulgey wood,
>   And burbled as it came!
>
> One, two! One, two! And through and through
>   The vorpal blade went snicker-snack!
> He left it dead, and with its head
>   He went galumphing back.
>
> "And hast thou slain the Jabberwock?
>   Come to my arms, my beamish boy!
> O frabjous day! Callooh! Callay!"
>   He chortled in his joy.
>
> 'Twas brillig, and the slithy toves
>   Did gyre and gimble in the wabe:
> All mimsy were the borogoves,
>   And the mome raths outgrabe.

Alice of course puzzled over this for a long time.

"'It seems very pretty,' she said when she had finished it, 'but it's rather hard to understand!' (You see she didn't like to confess, even to herself, that she couldn't make it out at all.) 'Somehow it seems to fill my head with ideas, only I don't exactly know what they are! However, *somebody* killed *something*—that's clear at any rate.'"

For pure cleverness the poem has no equal, we will not say in the English language, but in any language whatsoever, for it seems to be a medley of all languages. Lewis Carroll composed it on the spur of the moment during an evening spent with his cousins, the Misses Wilcox, and with his natural gift of word-making the result is most surprising. The only verse that really needs explanation is the first, which is also the last of the poem. Out of the twenty-three words the verse contains, there are but twelve which are pure, honest English.

In Mr. Collingwood's article in the *Strand Magazine* we have Lewis Carroll's explanation of the remaining eleven, written down in learned fashion, brimful of his own quaint humor. For a real guide it cannot be excelled, and, though we laugh at the absurdities, we learn the lesson. Here it is:

Brillig (derived from the verb to *bryl* or *broil*), "the time of broiling dinner—i. e., the close of the afternoon."

Slithy (compounded of slimy and lithe), "smooth and active."

Tove (a species of badger). "They had smooth, white hair, long hind legs, and short horns like a stag; lived chiefly on cheese."

Gyre (derived from Gayour or Giaour, a dog), "to scratch like a dog."

Gymble (whence Gimblet), "to screw out holes in anything."

Wabe (derived from the verb to swab or soak), "the side of a hill" (from its being *soaked* by the rain).

Mimsy (whence mimserable and miserable), "unhappy."

Borogove, "an extinct kind of parrot. They had no wings, beaks turned up, and made their nests under sun-dials; lived on veal."

Mome (hence solemome, solemne, and solemn), "grave."

Raths. "A species of land turtle, head erect, mouth like a shark; the forelegs curved out so that the animal walked on his knees; smooth green body; lived on swallows and oysters."

Outgrabe (past tense of the verb to outgribe; it is connected with the old verb to grike or shrike, from which are derived "shriek" and "creak"), "squeaked."

"Hence the literal English of the passage is—'It was evening, and the smooth active badgers were scratching and boring holes in the hillside; all unhappy were the parrots, and the green turtles squeaked out.' There were probably sun-dials on the top of the hill, and the borogoves were afraid that their nests would be undermined. The hill was probably full of the nests of 'raths' which ran out squeaking with fear on hearing the 'toves' scratching outside. This is an obscure yet deeply affecting relic of ancient poetry."

(Croft—1855. Ed.)

This lucid explanation was evidently one of the editor's contributions to *Misch-Masch* during his college days, so this classic poem must have "simmered" for many years before Lewis Carroll put it "Through the Looking-Glass." But when *Alice* questioned the all-wise *Humpty-Dumpty* on the subject he gave some simpler definitions. When asked the meaning of "mome raths," he replied:

"Well, *rath* is a sort of green pig; but *mome* I'm not certain about. I think it's short for 'from home,' meaning they'd lost their way, you know."

Lewis Carroll called such words "portmanteaus" because there were two meanings wrapped up in one word, and all through "Jabberwocky" these queer "portmanteau" words give us the key to the real meaning of the poem. In the preface to a collection of his poems, he gives us the rule for the building of these "portmanteau" words. He says: "Take the two words 'fuming' and 'furious.' Make up your mind that you will say both words, but leave it unsettled which you will say first. Now open your mouth and speak. If your thoughts incline ever so little toward 'fuming' you will say 'fuming-furious'; if they turn by even a hair's breadth toward 'furious' you will say 'furious-fuming'; but if you have that rarest of gifts, a perfectly balanced mind, you will say 'frumious.'"

It is hard to tell what he had in mind when he wrote of this deed of daring—for such it was. Possibly, St. George and the Dragon inspired him, and like the best of preachers he turned his sermon into wholesome nonsense. The Jabberwock itself was a most awe-inspiring creature, and Tenniel's drawing is most deliciously blood-curdling; half-snake, half-dragon, with "jaws that bite and claws that scratch," it is yet saved from being utterly terrible by having some nice homely looking buttons on his waistcoat and upon his three-clawed feet, something very near akin to shoes.

The anxious father bids his brave son good-bye, little dreaming that he will see him again.

> "Beware the Jubjub bird—and shun
> The frumious Bandersnatch"

are his last warning words, mostly "portmanteau" words, if one takes the time to puzzle them out. Then the brave boy goes forth into the "tulgey wood" and stands in "uffish thought" until with a "whiffling" sound the "burbling" Jabberwock is upon him.

Oh, the excitement of that moment when the "vorpal" sword went "snicker-snack" through the writhing neck of the monster! Then one can properly imagine the youth galloping in triumph (hence the "portmanteau" word "galumphing," the first syllable of gallop and the last syllable of triumph) back to the proud papa, who says: "Come to my arms, my 'beamish boy' ... and 'chortles in his joy.'" But all the time these wonderful things are happening, just around the corner, as it were, the "toves" and the "borogoves" and the "mome raths" were pursuing their never-ending warfare on the hillside, saying, with Tennyson's *Brook*:

> "Men may come and men may go—
> But *we* go on forever,"

no matter how many "Jabberwocks" are slain nor how many "beamish boys" take their "vorpal swords in hand."

In preparing the second "Alice" book for publication, Lewis Carroll's first idea was to use the "Jabberwocky" illustration as a frontispiece, but, in spite of the reassuring buttons and shoes, he was afraid younger children might be "scared off" from the real enjoyment of the book. So he wrote to about thirty mothers of small children asking their advice on the matter; they evidently voted against it, for, as we all know, the *White Knight* on his horse with its many trappings, with *Alice* walking beside him through the woods, was the final selection, and the smallest child has grown to love the silly old fellow who tumbled off his steed every two minutes, and did many other dear, ridiculous things that only children could appreciate.

Looking-glass walking puzzled *Alice* at first quite as much as looking-glass writing or reading. If she tried to walk downstairs in the looking-glass house "she just kept the tips of her fingers on the hand rail and floated gently down, without even touching the stairs with her feet." Then when she tried to climb to the top of the hill to get a peep into the garden, she found that she was always going backwards and in at the front door again. Finally, after many attempts, she reached the wished-for spot, and found herself among a talkative cluster of flowers, who all began to criticise her in the most impertinent way.

"Oh, Tiger-lily!" said Alice, addressing herself to one that was waving gracefully about in the wind, "I *wish* you could talk!"

"We can talk," said the Tiger-lily, "when there's anybody worth talking to" ... At length, as the Tiger-lily went on waving about, she spoke again in a timid voice, almost in a whisper:

"And can *all* the flowers talk?"

"As well as *you* can," said the Tiger-lily, "and a great deal louder."

"It isn't manners for us to begin, you know," said the Rose, "and I really was wondering when you'd speak! Said I to myself, 'Her face has got *some* sense in it though it's not a clever one!' Still you've the right color and that goes a long way."

"I don't care about the color," the Tiger-lily remarked. "If only her petals curled up a little more, she'd be all right."

Alice didn't like being criticised, so she began asking questions:

"Aren't you sometimes frightened at being planted out here with nobody to take care of you?"

"There's the tree in the middle," said the Rose. "What else is it good for?"

"But what could it do if any danger came?" Alice asked.

"It could bark," said the Rose.

"It says 'bough-wough'," cried a Daisy. "That's why its branches are called boughs."

"Didn't you know that?" cried another Daisy. And here they all began shouting together.

Lewis Carroll loved this play upon words, and children, strange to say, loved it too, and were quick to see the point of his puns. The *Red Queen*, whom *Alice* met shortly after this, was a most dictatorial person.

"Where do you come from?" she asked, "and where are you going? Look up, speak nicely, and don't twiddle your fingers all the time."

Alice attended to all these directions, and explained as well as she could that she had lost her way.

"I don't know what you mean by *your* way," said the Queen. "All the ways about here belong to *me*, but why did you come out here at all?" she added in a kinder tone. "Curtsey while you're thinking what to say. It saves time."

Alice wondered a little at this, but she was too much in awe of the Queen to disbelieve it.

"I'll try it when I go home," she thought to herself, "the next time I'm a little late for dinner."

Evidently some little girls were often late for dinner.

"It's time for you to answer now," the Queen said, looking at her watch; "open your mouth a *little* wider when you speak and always say 'Your Majesty.'"

"I only wanted to see what your garden was like, your Majesty."

"That's right," said the Queen, patting her on the head, which Alice didn't like at all, "though when you say 'garden,' *I've* seen gardens compared with which this would be a wilderness."

Alice didn't dare to argue the point, but went on: "And I thought I'd try and find my way to the top of that hill—"

"When you say 'hill,'" the Queen interrupted, "*I* could show you hills in comparison with which you'd call this a valley."

"No, I shouldn't," said Alice, surprised into contradicting her at last. "A hill *can't* be a valley you know. That would be nonsense—"

The *Red Queen* shook her head.

"You may call it 'nonsense' if you like," she said, "but *I've* heard nonsense compared with which that would be as sensible as a dictionary!"

Which last remark seemed to settle the matter, for *Alice* had nothing further to say on the subject.

Nonsense, indeed; and what delightful nonsense it is! Is it any wonder that the little girls for whom Lewis Carroll labored so lovingly should reward him with their laughter?

Alice entered Checker-Board Land in the *Red Queen's* company; she was apprenticed as a pawn, with the promise that when she entered the eighth square she would become a queen [she probably was confusing chess with checkers], and the *Red Queen* explained how she would travel.

"A pawn goes two squares in its first move, you know, so you'll go very quickly through the third square, by railway, I should think, and you'll find yourself in the fourth square in no time. Well, *that* square belongs to Tweedledum and Tweedledee, and the fifth is mostly water, the sixth belongs to Humpty Dumpty, ... the seventh square is all forest. However, one of the knights will show you the way, and in the eighth square we shall be queens together, and its all feasting and fun."

The rest of her adventures occurred on those eight squares— sometimes in company with the *Red Queen* or the *White Queen* or both. Things went more rapidly than in Wonderland, the people were brisker and smarter. When the *Red Queen* left her on the border of Checker-Board Land, she gave her this parting advice:

"Speak in French when you can't think of the English for a thing, turn out your toes as you walk, and remember who you are!"

How many little girls have had the same advice from their governesses or their mamma—"Turn out your toes when you walk, and remember who you are!"

This is what made Lewis Carroll so irresistibly funny—the way he had of bringing in the most common everyday expressions in the most uncommon, unexpected places. Only in *Alice's* case it took her quite a long time to remember who she was, just because the *Red Queen* told her not to forget. Children are very queer about that—little girls in particular—at least those that Lewis Carroll knew, and he certainly was acquainted with a great many who did remarkably queer things.

Alice's meeting with the two fat little men named *Tweedle-dum* and *Tweedledee* recalled to her memory the old rhyme:

> Tweedledum and Tweedledee
> > Agreed to have a battle;
> For Tweedledum said Tweedledee
> > Had spoiled his nice new rattle.
>
> Just then flew down a monstrous crow,
> > As black as a tar barrel;
> Which frightened both the heroes so,
> > They quite forgot their quarrel.

Fierce little men they were, one with *Dum* embroidered on his collar, the other showing *Dee* on his. They were not accustomed to good society nor fine grammar. They were exactly alike as they stood motionless before her, their arms about each other.

"I know what you're thinking about," said Tweedledum, "but it isn't so—nohow." [Behold the *beautiful* grammar.]

"Contrariwise," continued Tweedledee, "if it was so, it might be; and if it were so, it would be; but as it isn't, it ain't. That's logic."

Now, *Alice* particularly wanted to know which road to take out of the woods, but somehow or other her polite question was never answered by either of the funny little brothers. They were very sociable and seemed most anxious to keep her with them, so for her entertainment *Tweedledum* repeated that beautiful and pathetic poem called:

THE WALRUS AND THE CARPENTER

The sun was shining on the sea,
    Shining with all his might;
He did his very best to make
    The billows smooth and bright—
And this was odd, because it was
    The middle of the night.

The moon was shining sulkily,
    Because she thought the sun
Had got no business to be there
    After the day was done—
"It's very rude of him," she said,
    "To come and spoil the fun!"

The sea was wet as wet could be,
    The sands were dry as dry,
You could not see a cloud, because
    No cloud was in the sky;
No birds were flying overhead—
    There were no birds to fly.

The Walrus and the Carpenter
    Were walking close at hand;
They wept like anything to see
    Such quantities of sand;
"If this were only cleared away,"
    They said, "it *would* be grand!"

"If seven maids with seven mops
    Swept it for half a year,
Do you suppose," the Walrus said,
    "That they would get it clear?"
"I doubt it," said the Carpenter,
    And shed a bitter tear.

Then comes the sad and sober part of the tale, when the *Oysters* were tempted to stroll along the beach, in company with these wily two, who lured them far away from their snug ocean beds.

The Walrus and the Carpenter
    Walked on a mile or so,
And then they rested on a rock
    Conveniently low;
And all the little Oysters stood
    And waited in a row.

"The time has come," the Walrus said,
    "To talk of many things;
Of shoes, and ships, and sealing-wax—
    Of cabbages and kings;
And why the sea is boiling hot,
    And whether pigs have wings."

"But wait a bit," the Oysters cried,
    "Before we have our chat;
For some of us are out of breath,
    And all of us are fat!"
"No hurry!" said the Carpenter.
    They thanked him much for that.

"A loaf of bread," the Walrus said,
    "Is what we chiefly need;
Pepper and vinegar besides
    Are very good, indeed;
Now, if you're ready, Oysters, dear,
    We can begin to feed."

Then the *Oysters* became terrified, as they saw all these grewsome preparations, and their fate loomed up before them. So the two old weeping hypocrites sat on the rocks and calmly devoured their late companions.

> "It seems a shame," the Walrus said,
>   "To play them such a trick,
> After we've brought them out so far,
>   And made them trot so quick!"
> The Carpenter said nothing but,
>   "The butter's spread too thick!"
>
> "I weep for you," the Walrus said,
>   "I deeply sympathize."
> With sobs and tears he sorted out
>   Those of the largest size,
> Holding his pocket-handkerchief
>   Before his streaming eyes.
>
> "O Oysters," said the Carpenter,
>   "You've had a pleasant run!
> Shall we be trotting home again?"
>   But answer came there none.
> And this was scarcely odd, because
>   They'd eaten every one.

The poor dear little *Oysters*! How any little girl, with a heart under her pinafore, could read these lines unmoved it is hard to say. Think of those innocent young dears, standing before these dreadful ogres.

> All eager for the treat;
> Their coats were brushed, their faces washed,
>   Their shoes were clean and neat;
> And this was odd, because, you know,
>   They hadn't any feet.

All the same, Tenniel has made most attractive pictures of them, feet and all. And think—oh, horror! of *their* supplying the treat! It was indeed an awful tragedy. Yet behind it all there lurks some fun, though Lewis Carroll was too clever to let us *quite* into his secret. All the young ones want is the story, but those who are old enough to love their Dickens and to look for his special characters outside of his books will certainly recognize in the *Walrus* the hypocritical *Mr. Pecksniff*, whose tears flowed on every occasion when he was not otherwise employed in robbing his victims, and other little pleasantries. And as for the *Carpenter*, there is something very scholarly in the set of his cap and the combing of his scant locks; possibly a caricature of some shining light of Oxford, for we know there were many in his books. Indeed, the whole poem may be something of an allegory, representing examination; the *Oysters*, the undergraduate victims before the college faculty (the *Walrus* and the *Carpenter*) who are just ready to "eat 'em alive"—poor innocent undergraduates!

But whatever the hidden meaning, *Tweedledum* and *Tweedledee* were not the sort of people to look deep into things, and *Alice*, being a little girl and very partial to oysters, thought the *Walrus* and the *Carpenter* were *very* unpleasant characters and had no sympathy with them at all.

Dreaming by a ruddy blaze in a big armchair keeps one much busier than if one fell asleep in a rocking boat or on the river bank on a golden summer day.

The scenes and all the company changed so often in Looking-Glass Land that *Alice* had all she could do to keep pace with her adventures. For you see all this time she was only a pawn, moving over an immense chess-board from square to square, until in the end she should be made queen. The *White Queen* whom *Alice* met shortly was a very lopsided person, quite unlike the *Red Queen*, who was neat enough no matter how sharp her tongue. *Alice* had to fix her hair, and straighten her shawl, and set her right and tidy.

"Really, you should have a lady's maid," she remarked.

"I'm sure I'll take *you* with pleasure," the Queen said. "Twopence a week, and jam every other day."

Alice couldn't help laughing as she said:

"I don't want you to hire *me*, and I don't care for jam."

"It's very good jam," said the Queen.

"Well, I don't want any *to-day* at any rate."

"You couldn't have it if you *did* want it," the Queen said. "The rule is—jam to-morrow and jam yesterday, but never jam *to-day*."

"It *must* come sometimes to 'jam to-day,'" Alice objected.

"No, it can't," said the Queen. "It's jam every other day; to-day isn't any *other* day, you know."

"I don't understand you," said Alice. "It's dreadfully confusing!"

"That's the effect of living backwards," the Queen said, kindly. "It always makes one a little giddy at first—"

"Living backwards!" Alice remarked in great astonishment. "I never heard of such a thing!"

"But there's one great advantage in it, that one's memory works both ways."

"I'm sure *mine* only works one way," Alice remarked. "I can't remember things before they happen."

"It's a poor memory that only works backwards," the Queen remarked.

"What sort of things do *you* remember best?" Alice ventured to ask.

"Oh, the things that happened the week after next," the Queen replied in a careless tone. "For instance, now," she went on, sticking a large piece of plaster on her finger as she spoke, "there's the king's messenger. He's in prison now, being punished, and the trial doesn't begin till next Wednesday; and of course the crime comes last of all." Then the *Queen* for further illustration began to scream—

"Oh, oh, oh!" shouted the Queen.... "My finger's bleeding! Oh, oh, oh, oh!"

Her screams were so exactly like the whistle of a steam engine that Alice had to hold both her hands over her ears.

"What *is* the matter?" she said.... "Have you pricked your finger?"

"I haven't pricked it yet," the Queen said, "but I soon shall— oh, oh, oh!"

"When do you expect to do it?" Alice asked, feeling very much inclined to laugh.

"When I fasten my shawl again," the poor Queen groaned out, "the brooch will come undone directly. Oh, oh!" As she said the words the brooch flew open, and the Queen clutched wildly at it and tried to clasp it again.

"Take care!" cried Alice, "you're holding it all crooked!" and she caught at the brooch; but it was too late; the pin had slipped, and the Queen had pricked her finger.

"That accounts for the bleeding, you see," she said to Alice, with a smile. "Now you understand the way things happen here."

Alice's meeting with *Humpty-Dumpty* in the sixth square has gone down in history. It has been played in nurseries and in private theatricals, and many ingenious Humpty-Dumptys have been fashioned by clever people.

Possibly the dear old rhyme which generations of childhood have handed about as a riddle is responsible for our great interest in *Humpty-Dumpty*.

> Humpty-Dumpty sat on the wall,
> Humpty-Dumpty had a great fall,
> All the King's horses and all the King's men,
> Couldn't put Humpty-Dumpty in his place again.

This is an old version, but modern children have made a better ending, thus:

Couldn't put Humpty-Dumpty up again.

Then there's a mysterious pause, and some eager small boy or girl asks, "Now *what* is it?" and before one has time to answer, someone calls out—

"It's an egg; it's an egg!" and the riddle is a riddle no longer.

One clever mechanical Humpty was made of barrel hoops covered with stiff paper and muslin. The eyes, nose, and mouth were connected with various tapes, which the inventor had in charge behind the scenes, and so well did he work them that Humpty in his hands turned out a fine imitation of the *Humpty-Dumpty* Sir John Tenniel has made us remember; the same*Humpty-Dumpty* who asked *Alice* her name and her business, and who informed her proudly that if he did tumble off the wall, "*The King has promised me with his very own mouth—to—to—*"

"To send all his horses and all his men—" Alice interrupted rather unwisely.

"Now I declare that's too bad!" Humpty-Dumpty cried, breaking into a sudden passion. "You've been listening at doors, and behind trees, and down chimneys, or you wouldn't have known it."

"I haven't, indeed!" Alice said, very gently. "It's in a book."

"Ah, well! They may write such things in a *book*," Humpty-Dumpty said in a calmer tone. "That's what you call a History of England, that is. Now take a good look at me. I'm one that has spoken to a King, *I* am; mayhap you'll never see such another; and to show you I'm not proud you may shake hands with me...."

"Yes, all his horses and all his men," *Humpty-Dumpty* went on. "They'd pick me up in a minute, *they* would. However, this conversation is going on a little too fast; let's go back to the last remark but one."

Such a nice, common old chap is *Humpty-Dumpty*, so "stuck-up" because he has spoken to a King; and argue! Well, *Alice* never heard anything like it before, and found difficulty in keeping up a conversation that was disputed every step of the way. She found him worse than the *Cheshire Cat* or even the *Duchess* for that matter, and not half so well-bred.

He too favored *Alice* with the following poem, which he assured her was written entirely for her amusement, and here it is, with enough of Lewis Carroll's "nonsense" in it to let us know where it came from:

> In winter, when the fields are white,
> I sing this song for your delight:—
>
> In spring, when woods are getting green,
> I'll try and tell you what I mean:
>
> In summer, when the days are long,
> Perhaps you'll understand the song:
>
> In autumn, when the leaves are brown,
> Take pen and ink, and write it down.
>
> I sent a message to the fish:
> I told them: "This is what I wish."
>
> The little fishes of the sea,
> They sent an answer back to me.
>
> The little fishes' answer was:
> "We cannot do it, Sir, because——"
>
> I sent to them again to say:
> "It will be better to obey."
>
> The fishes answered, with a grin:
> "Why, what a temper you are in!"
>
> I told them once, I told them twice:
> They would not listen to advice.

> I took a kettle large and new,
> Fit for the deed I had to do.
>
> My heart went hop, my heart went thump:
> I filled the kettle at the pump.
>
> Then someone came to me and said:
> "The little fishes are in bed."
>
> I said to him, I said it plain:
> "Then you must wake them up again."
>
> I said it very loud and clear:
> I went and shouted in his ear.
>
> But he was very stiff and proud:
> He said: "You needn't shout so loud!"
>
> And he was very proud and stiff:
> He said: "I'd go and wake them, if——"
>
> I took a corkscrew from the shelf;
> I went to wake them up myself.
>
> And when I found the door was locked,
> I pulled and pushed and kicked and knocked.
>
> And when I found the door was shut,
> I tried to turn the handle, but——

With which highly satisfactory ending *Humpty* remarked:

"That's all. Good-bye."

Alice got up and held out her hand.

"Good-bye till we meet again," she said, as cheerfully as she could.

"I shouldn't know you if we *did* meet," Humpty-Dumpty replied in a discontented tone, giving her one of his fingers to shake. "You're so exactly like other people."

The next square—the seventh—took *Alice* through the woods. Here she met some old friends: the *Mad Hatter* and the *White Rabbit* of Wonderland fame, mixed in with a great many new beings, including the *Lion* and the *Unicorn*, who, as the old ballad tells us, "were fighting for the crown"; and then as the *Red Queen* had promised from the beginning, the *White Knight*—after a battle with the *Red Knight* who held *Alice* prisoner—took her in charge to guide her through the woods. Whoever has read the humorous and yet pathetic story of "Don Quixote" will see at once where Lewis Carroll found his gentle, valiant old *White Knight* and his horse, so like yet so unlike the famous steed *Rosenante*.

He, too, had a song for *Alice*, which he called "The Aged, Aged Man," and which he sang to her, set to very mechancholy music. It is doubtful if *Alice* understood it for she wasn't thinking of age, you see. She was only seven years and six months old, and probably paid no attention. She was thinking instead of the strange kindly smile of the knight, "the setting sun gleaming through his hair and shining on his armor in a blaze of light that quite dazzled her; the horse quietly moving about with the reins hanging loose on his neck, cropping the grass at her feet, and the black shadows of the forest behind." Certainly Lewis Carroll could paint a picture to remain with us always. The poem is rather too long to quote here, but the experiences of this "Aged, Aged Man" are well worth reading.

Alice was now hastening toward the end of her journey and events were tumbling over each other. She had reached the eighth square, where, oh, joy! a golden crown awaited her, also the *Red Queen* and the *White Queen* in whose company she traveled through the very stirring episodes of that very famous dinner party, when the candles on the table all grew up to the ceiling, and the glass bottles each took a pair of plates for wings, and forks for legs, and went fluttering in all directions. Everything was in the greatest confusion, and when the *White Queen* disappeared in the soup tureen, and the soup ladle began walking up the table toward *Alice's* chair, she could stand it no longer. She jumped up "and seized the tablecloth with both hands; one good pull, and plates, dishes, guests, and candles came crashing down together in a heap on the floor." And then *Alice* began to shake the *Red Queen* as the cause of all the mischief.

"The Red Queen made no resistance whatever; only her face grew very small, and her eyes got large and green; and still, as Alice went on shaking her, she kept on growing shorter, and fatter, and softer, and rounder, and—and it really *was* a kitten after all."

And *Alice*, opening her eyes in the red glow of the fire, lay snug in the armchair, while the Looking-Glass on the mantel caught the reflection of a very puzzled little face. The "dream-child" had come back to everyday, and was trying to retrace her journey as she lay there blinking at the firelight, and wondering if, back of the blaze, the Chessmen were still walking to and fro.

And Lewis Carroll, as he penned the last words of "Alice's Adventures through the Looking-Glass," remembered once more the little girl who had been his inspiration, and wrote a loving tribute to her at the very end of the book, an acrostic on her name—Alice Pleasance Liddell.

> A boat, beneath a sunny sky
> Lingering onward dreamily
> In an evening of July.
>
> Children three that nestle near,
> Eager eye and willing ear,
> Pleased a simple tale to hear.
>
> Long has paled that sunny sky;
> Echoes fade and memories die:
> Autumn frosts have slain July.
>
> Still she haunts me, phantomwise,
> Alice moving under skies,
> Never seen by waking eyes.

Children yet, the tale to hear,
Eager eye and willing ear,
Lovingly shall nestle near.

In a Wonderland they lie,
Dreaming as the days go by,
Dreaming as the summers die:

Ever drifting down the stream,
Lingering in the golden gleam,
Life, what is it but a dream?

Chapter X

'Hunting the Snark' and Other Poems

There is no doubt that the second "Alice" book was quite as successful as the first, but regarding its merit there is much difference of opinion. As a rule the "grown-ups" prefer it. They like the clever situations and the quaint logic, no less than the very evident good writing; but this of course did not influence the children in the least. They liked "Alice" and the pretty idea of her trip through the Looking-Glass, but for real delight "Wonderland" was big enough for them, and to whisk down into a rabbit-hole on a summer's day was a much easier process than squeezing through a looking-glass at the close of a short winter's afternoon, not being *quite* sure that one would not fall into the fire on the other side.

The very care that Lewis Carroll took in the writing of this book deprived it of a certain charm of originality which always clings to the pages of "Wonderland." Each chapter is so methodically planned and so well carried out that, while we never lose sight of the author and his cleverness, fairyland does not seem quite so real as in the book which was written with no plan at all, but the earnest desire to please three children. Then again there was a certain staidness in the prim little girl who pushed her way through the Looking-Glass. And there were no wonderful cakes marked "eat me," and bottles marked "drink me," which kept the Wonderland *Alice* in a perpetual state of growing or shrinking; so the fact that nothing happened to *Alice* at all during this second journey lessened its interest somewhat for the young ones to whom constant change is the spice of life. A very little girl, while she might enjoy the flower chapter, and might be tempted to build her own fanciful tales about the rest of the garden, would not be so attracted toward the insect chapter, which may possibly have been written with the praiseworthy idea of teaching children not to be afraid of these harmless buzzing things that are too busy with their own concerns to bother them.

There are, in truth, little "cut and dried" speeches in the Looking-Glass "Alice," which we do not find in "Wonderland." A real hand is moving the Chessman over the giant board, and the *Red* and the *White Queen* often speak like automatic toys. We miss the savage "off with his head" of the *Queen of Hearts*, who, for all her cardboard stiffness, seemed a thing of flesh and blood. But the poetry in the two "Alices" is of very much the same quality.

In his prose "nonsense" anyone might notice the difference of years between the two books, but Lewis Carroll's poetry never loses its youthful tone. It was as easy for him to write verses as to teach mathematics, and that was saying a good deal. It was as easy for him to write verses at sixty as at thirty, and that is saying even more. From the time he could hold a pencil he could make a rhyme, and his earlier editorial ventures, as we know, were full of his own work which in after years made its way to the public, either through the magazines or in collection of poems, such as "Rhyme and Reason," "Phantasmagoria," and "The Three Sunsets."

In *The Train*, that early English magazine before mentioned, are several poems written by him and signed by his newly borrowed name of Lewis Carroll, but they are very sentimental and high-flown, utterly unlike anything he wrote either before or after.

Between the publication of "Through the Looking-Glass" and "The Hunting of the Snark" was a period of five years, during which, according to his usual custom, Charles Lutwidge Dodgson, in the seclusion of Christ Church, calmly pursued his scholarly way, smiling sedately over the literary antics of Lewis Carroll, for the Rev. Charles was a sober, over-serious bachelor, whose one aim and object at that time was the proper treatment of Euclid, for during those five years he wrote the following pamphlets: "Symbols, etc., to be used in Euclid—Books I and II," "Number of Propositions in Euclid," "Enunciations—Euclid I-VI," "Euclid—Book V. Proved Algebraically," "Preliminary Algebra and Euclid—Book V," "Examples in Arithmetic," "Euclid—Books I and II."

He also wrote many other valuable pamphlets concerning the government of Oxford and of Christ Church in particular, for the retiring "don" took a keen interest in the University life, and his influence was felt in many spicy articles and apt rhymes, usually brought forth as timely skits. *Notes by an Oxford Chiel*, published at Oxford in 1874, included much of this material, where his clever verses, mostly satirical, generally hit the mark.

And all this while, Lewis Carroll was gathering in the harvest yielded by the two "Alices," and planning more books for his child-friends, who, we may be sure, were growing in numbers.

We find him at the Christmas celebration of 1874, at Hatfield, the home of Lord Salisbury, as usual, the central figure of a crowd of happy children. On this occasion he told them the story of *Prince Uggug*, which was afterwards a part of "Sylvie and Bruno." Many of the chapters of this book had been published as separate stories in *Aunt Judy's Magazine* and other periodicals, and, as such, they were very sweet and dainty as well as amusing. It was Lewis Carroll's own special charm in telling these stories which really lent them color and drew the children; they lost much in print, for they lacked the sturdy foundations of nonsense on which the "Alices" were built.

On March 29, 1876, "The Hunting of the Snark" was published, a new effort in "nonsense" verse-making, which stands side by side with "Jabberwocky" in point of cleverness and interest.

The beauty of Lewis Carroll's "nonsense" was that he never tried to be funny or "smart." The queer words and the still queerer ideas popped into his head in the simplest way. His command of language, including that important knowledge of how to make "portmanteau" words, was his greatest aid, and the poem which he called "An Agony in Eight Fits" depends entirely upon the person who reads it for the cleverness of its meaning. To children it is one big fairy tale where the more ridiculous the situations, the more true to the rules of fairyland. The Snark, being a "portmanteau" word, is a cross between a *snake* and a *shark*, hence *Snark*, and the fact that he dedicated this wonderful bit of word-making to a little girl, goes far to prove that the poem was intended as much for children as for "grown-ups."

The little girl in this instance was Gertrude Chataway, and the verses are an acrostic on her name:

> Girt with a boyish garb for boyish task,
>   Eager she wields her spade: yet loves as well
> Rest on a friendly knee, intent to ask
>   The tale he loves to tell.
>
> Rude spirit of the seething outer strife,
>   Unmeet to read her pure and simple spright,
> Deem, if you list, such hours a waste of life,
>   Empty of all delight!
>
> Chat on, sweet maid, and rescue from annoy,
>   Hearts that by wiser talk are unbeguiled;
> Ah, happy he who owns that tenderest joy,
>   The heart-love of a child!
>
> Away, fond thoughts, and vex my soul no more!
>   Work claims my wakeful nights, my busy days,
> Albeit bright memories of that sunlit shore
>   Yet haunt my dreaming gaze!

There was scarcely a little girl who claimed friendship with Lewis Carroll who was not the proud possessor of an acrostic poem written by him—either on the title-page of some book that he had given her, or as the dedication of some published book of his own.

"The Hunting of the Snark" owed its existence to a country walk, when the last verse came suddenly into the mind of our poet:

> "In the midst of the word he was trying to say,
>   In the midst of his laughter and glee,
> He had softly and suddenly vanished away—
>   For the Snark was a Boojum, you see."

In a very humorous preface to the book, Lewis Carroll attempted some sort of an explanation, which leaves us as much in the dark as ever. He writes:

"If—and the thing is wildly possible—the charge of writing nonsense was ever brought against the author of this brief but instructive poem, it would be based, I feel convinced, on the line:

"'Then the bowsprit got mixed with the rudder sometimes.'

"In view of this painful possibility, I will not (as I might) appeal indignantly to my other writings as a proof that I am incapable of such a deed; I will not (as I might) point to the strong moral purpose of the poem itself, to the arithmetical principles so cautiously inculcated in it, or to its noble teachings in Natural History. I will take the more prosaic course of simply explaining how it happened.

"The Bellman, who was almost morbidly sensitive about appearances, used to have the bowsprit unshipped once or twice a week to be revarnished; and more than once it happened, when the time came for replacing it, that no one on board could remember which end of the ship it belonged to. They knew it was not of the slightest use to appeal to the Bellman about it—he would only refer to his Naval Code and read out in pathetic tones Admiralty Instructions which none of them had ever been able to understand, so it generally ended in its being fastened on anyhow across the rudder. The Helmsman used to stand by with tears in his eyes; *he* knew it was all wrong, but, alas! Rule 4, of the Code, '*No one shall speak to the man at the helm*,' had been completed by the Bellman himself with the words, '*and the man at the helm shall speak to no one*,' so remonstrance was impossible and no steering could be done till the next varnishing day. During these bewildering intervals the ship usually sailed backward."

Is it any wonder that a poem, based upon such an explanation, should be a perfect bundle of nonsense? But we know from experience that Lewis Carroll's nonsense was not stupidity, and that not one verse in all that delightful bundle missed its own special meaning and purpose.

We do not propose to find the key to this remarkable work—for two reasons: first, because there are different keys for different minds; and second, because the unexplainable things in many cases come nearer the "mind's eye," as Shakespeare calls it, without words. We cannot tell *why* we understand such and such a thing, but we *do* understand it, and that is enough—quite according to Lewis Carroll's ideas, for he always appeals to our imagination and that is never guided by rules. The higher it soars, the more fantastic the region over which it hovers, the nearer it gets to the land of "make believe," "let's pretend" and "supposing," the better pleased is Lewis Carroll. In a delightful letter to some American children, published in *The Critic* shortly after his death, he gives his own ideas as to the meaning of the *Snark*.

"I'm very much afraid I didn't mean anything but nonsense," he wrote; "still you know words mean more than we mean to express when we use them, so a whole book ought to mean a great deal more than the writer means. So whatever good meanings are in the book, I shall be glad to accept as the meaning of the book. The best that I've seen is by a lady (she published it in a letter to a newspaper) that the whole book is an allegory on the search after happiness. I think this fits beautifully in many ways, particularly about the bathing machines; when people get weary of life, and can't find happiness in towns or in books, then they rush off to the seaside to see what bathing machines will do for them."

Taking this idea for the foundation of the poem, it is easy to explain *Fit the First*, better named *The Landing*, though where they landed it is almost impossible to say.

"Just the place for a Snark," the Bellman cried, and, as he stated this fact three distinct times, it was undoubtedly true. That was the *Bellman's* rule—once was uncertain, twice was possible, three times was "dead sure." And the *Bellman* being a person of some authority, ought to have known. The crew consisted of a *Boots*, a *Maker of Bonnets and Hoods*, a *Barrister*, a *Broker*, a *Billiard-marker*, a *Banker*, a *Beaver*, a *Butcher*, and a nameless being who passed for the *Baker*, and who, in the end, turned out to be the luckless victim of the Snark. He is thus beautifully described:

"There was one who was famed for a number of things
    He forgot when he entered the ship:
His umbrella, his watch, all his jewels and rings,
    And the clothes he had brought for the trip.

"He had forty-two boxes, all carefully packed,
    With his name painted clearly on each:
But, since he omitted to mention the fact,
    They were all left behind on the beach.

"The loss of his clothes hardly mattered, because
    He had seven coats on when he came,
With three pair of boots—but the worst of it was,
    He had wholly forgotten his name.

"He would answer to 'Hi!' or to any loud cry,
    Such as 'Fry me!' or 'Fritter my wig!'
To 'What-you-may-call-um!' or 'What-was-his-name!'
    But especially 'Thing-um-a-jig!'

"While, for those who preferred a more forcible word,
    He had different names from these:
His intimate friends called him 'Candle-ends,'
    And his enemies 'Toasted-cheese.'

"'His form is ungainly, his intellect small'
    (So the Bellman would often remark);
'But his courage is perfect! and that, after all,
    Is the thing that one needs with a Snark.'

"He would joke with hyenas, returning their stare
    With an impudent wag of the head:
And he once went a walk, paw-in-paw with a bear,
    'Just to keep up its spirits,' he said.

"He came as a Baker: but owned when too late—
    And it drove the poor Bellman half-mad—

> He could only bake Bride-cake, for which I may state,
>   No materials were to be had."

Notice how ingeniously the actors in this drama are introduced; all the "B's," as it were, buzzing after the phantom of happiness, which eludes them, no matter how hard they struggle to find it. Notice, too, that all these beings are unmarried, a fact shown by the *Baker* not being able to make a bride-cake as there are no materials on hand. All these creatures, while hunting for happiness, came to prey upon each other. The *Butcher* only killed *Beavers*, the *Barrister* was hunting among his fellow sailors for a good legal case. The *Banker* took charge of all their cash, for it certainly takes money to hunt properly for a *Snark*, and it is a well-known fact that bankers need all the money they can get.

Fit the Second describes the *Bellman* and why he had such influence with his crew:

> The Bellman himself they all praised to the skies:
>   Such a carriage, such ease, and such grace!
> Such solemnity, too! One could see he was wise,
>   The moment one looked in his face!
>
> He had bought a large map representing the sea,
>   Without the least vestige of land:
> And the crew were much pleased when they found it to be
>   A map they could all understand.
>
> "What's the good of Mercator's North Poles and Equators,
>   Tropics, Zones, and Meridian Lines?"
> So the Bellman would cry: and the crew would reply,
>   "They are merely conventional signs!"
>
> "Other maps are such shapes, with their islands and capes!
>   But we've got our brave Captain to thank"
> (So the crew would protest), "that he's bought *us* the best—
>   A perfect and absolute blank!"

And true enough, the *Bellman's* idea of the ocean was a big square basin, with the latitude and longitude carefully written out on the margin. They found, however, that their "brave Captain" knew very little about navigation, he—

"Had only one notion for crossing the ocean, And that was to tingle his bell."

He thought nothing of telling his crew to steer starboard and larboard at the same time, and then we know how—

The bowsprit got mixed with the rudder sometimes.
    "A thing," as the Bellman remarked,
"That frequently happens in tropical climes,
    When a vessel is, so to speak, 'snarked.'"

The *Bellman* had hoped, when the wind blew toward the east, that the ship would not travel toward the west, but it seems that with all his nautical knowledge he could not prevent it; ships are perverse animals!

"But the danger was past—they had landed at last,
    With their boxes, portmanteaus, and bags:
Yet at first sight the crew were not pleased with the view,
    Which consisted of chasms and crags."

Now that they had reached the land of the Snark, the *Bellman* proceeded to air his knowledge on that subject.

"A snark," he said, "had five unmistakable traits—its taste, 'meager and mellow and crisp,' its habit of getting up late, its slowness in taking a jest, its fondness for bathing machines, and, fifth and lastly, its ambition." He further informed the crew that "the snarks that had feathers could bite, and those that had whiskers could scratch," adding as an afterthought:

"'For although common Snarks do no manner of harm,
    Yet I feel it my duty to say,
Some are Boojums—' The Bellman broke off in alarm,
    For the Baker had fainted away."

Fit the Third was the *Baker's* tale.

"They roused him with muffins, they roused him with ice,
    They roused him with mustard and cress,
They roused him with jam and judicious advice,
    They set him conundrums to guess."

Then he explained why it was that the name "Boojum" made him faint. It seems that a dear uncle, after whom he was named, gave him some wholesome advice about the way to hunt a snark, and this uncle seemed to be a man of much influence:

"'You may seek it with thimbles, and seek it with care;
    You may hunt it with forks and hope;
You may threaten its life with a railway-share;
    You may charm it with smiles and soap——'"

"'That's exactly the method,' the Bellman bold
    In a hasty parenthesis cried,
'That's exactly the way I have always been told
    That the capture of Snarks should be tried!'"

"'But, oh, beamish nephew, beware of the day,
    If your Snark be a Boojum! For then
You will softly and suddenly vanish away,
    And never be met with again!'"

This of course was a very sad thing to think of, for the man with no name, who was named after his uncle, and called in courtesy the *Baker*, had grown to be a great favorite with the crew; but they had no time to waste in sentiment—they were in the Snark's own land, they had the *Bellman's* orders in *Fit the Fourth*—the Hunting:

"To seek it with thimbles, to seek it with care;
    To pursue it with forks and hope;
To threaten its life with a railway share;
    To charm it with smiles and soap!

"For the Snark's a peculiar creature, that won't
    Be caught in a commonplace way.

Do all that you know, and try all that you don't:
>Not a chance must be wasted to-day!"

Then they all went to work according to their own special way, just as we would do now in our hunt for happiness through the chasms and crags of every day.

Fit the Fifth is the *Beaver's* Lesson, when the *Butcher* discourses wisely on arithmetic and natural history, two subjects a butcher should know pretty thoroughly, and this is proved:

>"While the Beaver confessed, with affectionate looks
>>More eloquent even than tears,
>It had learned in ten minutes far more than all books
>>Would have taught it in seventy years."

The *Barrister's* Dream occupied *Fit the Sixth*, and here our poet's keen wit gave many a slap at the law and the lawyers.

The *Banker's* Fate in *Fit the Seventh* was sad enough; he was grabbed by the Bandersnatch (that "frumious" "portmanteau" creature that we met before in the *Lay of the Jabberwocky*) and worried and tossed about until he completely lost his senses. Some bankers are that way in the pursuit of fortune, which means happiness to them; but fortune may turn, like the Bandersnatch, and shake their minds out of their bodies, and so they left this *Banker* to his fate. That is the way of people when bankers are in trouble, because they were reckless and not always careful to

>"Beware the Jubjub bird, and shun
>The frumious Bandersnatch."

Fit the Eighth treats of the vanishing of the Baker according to the prediction of his prophetic uncle. All day long the eager searchers had hunted in vain, but just at the close of the day they heard a shout in the distance and beheld their *Baker* "erect and sublime" on top of a crag, waving his arms and shouting wildly; then before their startled and horrified gaze, he plunged into a chasm and disappeared forever.

> "'It's a Snark!' was the sound that first came to their ears,
>   And seemed almost too good to be true.
> Then followed a torrent of laughter and cheers,
>   Then the ominous words, 'It's a Boo——'
>
> "Then, silence. Some fancied they heard in the air
>   A weary and wandering sigh
> That sounded like 'jum!' but the others declare
>   It was only a breeze that went by.
>
> "They hunted till darkness came on, but they found
>   Not a button, or feather, or mark
> By which they could tell that they stood on the ground
>   Where the Baker had met with the Snark.
>
> "In the midst of the word he was trying to say,
>   In the midst of his laughter and glee,
> He had softly and suddenly vanished away—
>   For the Snark was a Boojum, you see."

What became of the *Bellman* and his crew is left to our imagination. Perhaps the *Baker's* fate was a warning, or perhaps they are still hunting—not *too* close to the chasm. Lewis Carroll, always so particular about proper endings, refuses any explanation. The fact that this special Snark was a "Boojum" altered all the rules of the hunt. Nobody knows what it is, but all the same nobody wishes to meet a "Boojum." That's all there is about it.

"Now how absurd to talk such nonsense!" some learned school girl may exclaim; undoubtedly one who has high ideals about life and literature. But is it nonsense we are talking, and does the quaint poem really teach us nothing? Anything which brings a picture to the mind must surely have some merit, and there is much homely common sense wrapped up in the queer verses if we have but the wit to find it, and no one is too young nor too old to join in this hunt for happiness.

Read the poem over and over, put expression and feeling into it, treat the *Bellman* and his strange crew as if they were real human beings—there's a lot of the human in them after all—and see if new ideas and new meanings do not pop into your head with each reading, while the verses, all unconsciously, will stick in your memory, where Tennyson or Wordsworth or even Shakespeare fails to hold a place there.

Of course, Lewis Carroll's own especial girlfriends understood "The Hunting of the Snark" better than the less favored "outsiders." First of all there was Lewis Carroll himself to read it to them in his own expressive way, his pleasant voice sinking impressively at exciting moments, and his clear explanation of each "portmanteau" word helping along wonderfully. We can fancy the gleam of fun in the blue eyes, the sweep of his hand across his hair, the sudden sweet smile with which he pointed his jests or clothed his moral, as the case might be. Indeed, one little girl was so fascinated with the poem which he sent her as a gift that she learned the whole of it by heart, and insisted on repeating it during a long country drive.

"The Hunting of the Snark" created quite a sensation among his friends. The first edition was finely illustrated by Henry Holiday, whose clever drawings show how well he understood the poem, and what sympathy existed between himself and the author.

"Phantasmagoria," his ghost poem, deals with the friendly relations always existing between ghosts and the people they are supposed to haunt; a whimsical idea, carried out in Lewis Carroll's whimsical way, with lots of fun and a good deal of simple philosophy worked out in the verses. One canto is particularly amusing. Here are some of the verses:

> Oh, when I was a little Ghost,
>   A merry time had we!
>   Each seated on his favorite post,
> We chumped and chawed the buttered toast
>   They gave us for our tea.
>
> "That story is in print!" I cried.
>   "Don't say it's not, because
>   It's known as well as Bradshaw's Guide!"

(The Ghost uneasily replied
  He hardly thought it was.)

It's not in Nursery Rhymes? And yet
  I almost think it is—
  "Three little Ghostesses" were set
"On postesses," you know, and ate
  Their "buttered toastesses."

"The Three Voices," his next ambitious poem, is rather out of the realm of childhood. A weak-minded man and a strong-minded lady met on the seashore, she having rescued his hat from the antics of a playful breeze by pinning it down on the sands with her umbrella, right through the center of the soft crown. When she handed it to him in its battered state, he was scarcely as grateful as he might have been—he was rude, in fact,

For it had lost its shape and shine,
And it had cost him four-and-nine,
And he was going out to dine.

"To dine!" she sneered in acid tone.
"To bend thy being to a bone
Clothed in a radiance not its own!"

"Term it not 'radiance,'" said he:
"'Tis solid nutriment to me.
Dinner is Dinner: Tea is Tea."

And she "Yea so? Yet wherefore cease?
Let thy scant knowledge find increase.
Say 'Men are Men, and Geese are Geese.'"

The gentleman wanted to get away from this severe lady, but he could see no escape, for she was getting excited.

"To dine!" she shrieked, in dragon-wrath.
"To swallow wines all foam and froth!
To simper at a tablecloth!

"Canst thou desire or pie or puff?
Thy well-bred manners were enough,
Without such gross material stuff."

"Yet well-bred men," he faintly said,
"Are not unwilling to be fed:
Nor are they well without the bread."

Her visage scorched him ere she spoke;
"There are," she said, "a kind of folk
Who have no horror of a joke.

"Such wretches live: they take their share
Of common earth and common air:
We come across them here and there."

"We grant them—there is no escape—
A sort of semihuman shape
Suggestive of the manlike Ape."

So the arguing went on—her Voice, his Voice, and the Voice of
the Sea. He tried to joke away her solemn mood with a pun.

"The world is but a Thought," said he:
"The vast, unfathomable sea
Is but a Notion—unto me."

And darkly fell her answer dread
Upon his unresisting head,
Like half a hundredweight of lead.

"The Good and Great must ever shun
That reckless and abandoned one
Who stoops to perpetrate a pun.

"The man that smokes—that reads the Times—
That goes to Christmas Pantomimes—
Is capable of any crimes!"

Anyone can understand these verses, but it is very plain that the poem is a satire on the rise of the learned lady, who takes no interest in the lighter, pleasanter side of life; a being much detested by Lewis Carroll, who above all things loved a "womanly woman." As he grew older he became somewhat precise and old-fashioned in his opinions—that is perhaps the reason why he was so lovable. His ideals of womanhood and little girlhood were fixed and beautiful dreams, untouched by the rush of the times. The "new woman" puzzled and pained him quite as much as the pert, precocious, up-to-date girl. Would there were more Lewis Carrolls in the world; quiet, simple, old-fashioned, courteous gentlemen with ideals!

Here is a clever little poem dedicated to girls, which he calls

A GAME OF FIVES

Five little girls, of five, four, three, two, one:
Rolling on the hearthrug, full of tricks and fun.

Five rosy girls, in years from ten to six:
Sitting down to lessons—no more time for tricks.

Five growing girls, from fifteen to eleven:
Music, drawing, languages, and food enough for seven!

Five winsome girls, from twenty to sixteen:
Each young man that calls I say, "Now tell me which
    you mean!"

Five dashing girls, the youngest twenty-one:
But if nobody proposes, what is there to be done?

Five showy girls—but thirty is an age
When girls may be engaging, but they somehow don't en-
    gage.

Five dressy girls, of thirty-one or more:
So gracious to the shy young men they snubbed so much
    before!

Five passé girls. Their age? Well, never mind!
We jog along together, like the rest of human kind:

But the quondam "careless bachelor" begins to think he
 knows
The answer to that ancient problem "how the money goes!"

There was no theme, in short, that Lewis Carroll did not fit into a rhyme or a poem. Some of them were full of real feeling, others were sparkling with nonsense, but all had their charm. No style nor meter daunted him; no poet was too great for his clever pen to parody; no ode was too heroic for a little earthly fun; and when the measure was rollicking the rhymer was at his best. Of this last, *Alice's* invitation to the Looking-Glass world is a fair example:

To the Looking-Glass world it was Alice that said,
"I've a scepter in hand, I've a crown on my head.
Let the Looking-Glass creatures, whatever they be,
Come and dine with the Red Queen, the White Queen,
 and me!"

> Then fill up the glasses as quick as you can,
> And sprinkle the table with buttons and bran;
> Put cats in the coffee, and mice in the tea,
> And welcome Queen Alice with thirty-times-three!

"O Looking-Glass creatures," quoth Alice, "draw near!
'Tis an honor to see me, a favor to hear;
'Tis a privilege high to have dinner and tea
Along with the Red Queen, the White Queen, and me!"

> Then fill up the glasses with treacle and ink,
> Or anything else that is pleasant to drink;
> Mix sand with the cider, and wool with the wine,
> And welcome Queen Alice with ninety-times-nine!

The real sentiment always cropped out in his verses to little girls; from youth to age he was their "good knight and true" and all his fairest thoughts were kept for them. Many a grown woman has carefully hoarded among her treasures some bit of verse from Lewis Carroll, which her happy childhood inspired him to write; but the dedication of "Alice through the Looking-Glass" was to the unknown child, whom his book went forth to please:

> Child of the pure, unclouded brow
> And dreaming eyes of wonder!
> Though time be fleet, and I and thou
> Are half a life asunder,
> Thy loving smile will surely hail
> The love-gift of a fairy tale.
>
> I have not seen thy sunny face,
> Nor heard thy silver laughter:
> No thought of me shall find a place
> In thy young life's hereafter,
> Enough that now thou wilt not fail
> To listen to my fairy tale.
>
> A tale begun in other days,
> When summer suns were glowing,
> A simple chime, that served to time
> The rhythm of our rowing,
> Whose echoes live in memory yet,
> Though envious years would say "forget."
>
> Come, hearken then, ere voice of dread,
> With bitter tidings laden,
> Shall summon to unwelcome bed
> A melancholy maiden!
> We are but older children, dear,
> Who fret to find our bedtime near.
>
> Without, the frost, the blinding snow,
> The storm-wind's moody madness;
> Within, the firelight's ruddy glow,
> And childhood's nest of gladness.

The magic words shall hold thee fast;
Thou shalt not heed the raving blast.

And though the shadow of a sigh
    May tremble through the story,
For "happy summer days" gone by
    And vanished summer glory,
It shall not touch, with breath of bale,
The pleasance of our fairy tale.

These are only a meager handful of his many poems. Through his life this gift stayed with him, with all its early spirit and freshness; the added years but added grace and lightness to his touch, for in the "Story of Sylvie and Bruno" there are some gems: but that is another chapter and we shall hear them later.

And so the years passed, and the writer of the "Alices" and the "Jabberwocky" and "The Hunting of the Snark" and other poems fastened himself slowly but surely into the loyal hearts of his many readers, and the grave mathematical lecturer of Christ Church seemed just a trifle older and graver than of yore. He was very reserved, very shy, and kept somewhat aloof from his fellow "dons"; but let a little girl tap *ever* so faintly at his study door, the knock was heard, the door flung wide, Charles Lutwidge Dodgson vanished into some inner sanctum, and Lewis Carroll stood smiling on the threshold to welcome her with open arms.

Chapter XI

Games, Riddles, and Problems

Lewis Carroll had a mind which never rested in waking hours, and as is the case with all such active thinkers, his hours of sleeping were often broken by long stretches of wakefulness, during which time the thinking machinery set itself in motion and spun out problems and riddles and odd games and puzzles.

"Puzzles and problems of all sorts were a delight to Mr. Dodgson," writes Miss Beatrice Hatch in the *Strand Magazine*. "Many a sleepless night was occupied by what he called a 'pillow problem'; in fact his mathematical mind seemed always at work on something of the kind, and he loved to discuss and argue a point connected with his logic, if he could but find a willing listener. Sometimes, while paying an afternoon call, he would borrow scraps of paper and leave neat little diagrams or word puzzles to be worked out by his friends."

Logic was a study of which he was very fond. After he gave up in 1881 the lectureship of mathematics which he had held for twenty-five years he determined to make literature a profession; to devote part of his time to more serious study, and a fair portion to the equally fascinating work for children.

"In his estimation," says Miss Hatch, "logic was a most important study for every one; no pains were spared to make it clear and interesting to those who would consent to learn of him, either in a class that he begged to be allowed to hold in a school or college, or to a single individual girl who showed the smallest inclination to profit by his instructions."

He took the greatest delight in his subject and wisely argued that all girls should learn, not only to reason, but to reason properly—that is, logically. With this end in view he wrote for their use a little book which he called "The Game of Logic," and the girls, whose footsteps he had guided in childish days through realms of nonsense, were willing in many instances to journey with him into the byways of learning, feeling sure he would not lead them into depths where they could not follow. The little volume contains four chapters, and the whimsical headings show us at once that Lewis Carroll was the author, and not Charles Lutwidge Dodgson.

Chapter I.........New Lamps for Old.
Chapter II.......Cross Questions.
Chapter III......Crooked Answers.
Chapter IV......Hit or Miss.

To be sure this is not a "play" book, and even as a "game" it is one which requires a great deal of systematic thinking and reasoning. The girl who has reached thinking and reasoning years and does not care to do either, had better not even peep into the book; but if she is built on sturdier lines and wishes to peep, she must do more—she must read it step by step and study the carefully drawn diagrams, if she would follow intelligently the clear, precise arguments. The book is dedicated—

TO MY CHILD-FRIEND

I charm in vain: for never again,
All keenly as my glance I bend,
  Will memory, goddess coy,
  Embody for my joy
Departed days, nor let me gaze
  On thee, my Fairy Friend!

Yet could thy face, in mystic grace,
A moment smile on me, 'twould send
  Far-darting rays of light
  From Heaven athwart the night,
By which to read in very deed
  Thy spirit, sweetest Friend!

So may the stream of Life's long dream
Flow gently onward to its end,
With many a floweret gay,
Adown its billowy way:
May no sigh vex nor care perplex
My loving little Friend!

His preface is most enticing. He says: "This Game requires nine Counters—four of one color and five of another; say four red and five gray. Besides the nine Counters, it also requires one Player *at least*. I am not aware of any game that can be played with *less* than this number; while there are several that require more; take Cricket, for instance, which requires twenty-two. How much easier it is, when you want to play a game, to find *one* Player than twenty-two! At the same time, though one Player is enough, a good deal more amusement may be got by two working at it together, and correcting each other's mistakes.

"A second advantage possessed by this Game is that, besides being an endless source of amusement (the number of arguments that may be worked by it being infinite), it will give the Players a little instruction as well. But is there any great harm in that, so long as you get plenty of amusement?"

To explain the book thoroughly would take the wit and clever handling of Lewis Carroll himself, but to the beginner of Logic a few of these unfinished syllogisms may prove interesting: a syllogism in logical language consists of what is known as two *Premisses* and one *Conclusion*, and is a very simple form of argument when you get used to it.

For instance, supposing someone says: "All my friends have colds"; someone else may add: "No one can sing who has a cold"; then the third person draws the conclusion, which is: "None of my friends can sing," and the perfect logical argument would read as follows:

1. Premise—"All my friends have colds."
2. Premise—"No one can sing who has a cold."
3. Conclusion—"None of my friends can sing."

That is what is called a perfect syllogism, and in Chapter IV, which he calls *Hit or Miss*, Lewis Carroll has collected a hundred examples containing the two *Premisses* which need the *Conclusion*. Here are some of them. Anyone can draw her own conclusions:

> Pain is wearisome;
> No pain is eagerly wished for.

In each case the student is required to fill up the third space.

> No bald person needs a hairbrush;
> No lizards have hair.

> No unhappy people chuckle;
> No happy people groan.

> All ducks waddle;
> Nothing that waddles is graceful.

> Some oysters are silent;
> No silent creatures are amusing.

> Umbrellas are useful on a journey;
> What is useless on a journey should be left behind.

> No quadrupeds can whistle;
> Some cats are quadrupeds.

> Some bald people wear wigs;
> All your children have hair.

The whole book is brimful of humor and simple everyday reasoning that the smallest child could understand.

Another "puzzle" book of even an earlier date is "A Tangled Tale"; this is dedicated—

TO MY PUPIL

> Belovéd pupil! Tamed by thee,
>   Addish, Subtrac-, Multiplica-tion,
> Division, Fractions, Rule of Three,
>   Attest the deft manipulation!

Then onward! Let the voice of Fame,
From Age to Age repeat the story,
Till thou hast won thyself a name,
Exceeding even Euclid's glory!

In the preface he says: "This Tale originally appeared as a serial in *The Monthly Packet*, beginning in April, 1880. The writer's intention was to embody in each Knot (like the medicine so deftly but ineffectually concealed in the jam of our childhood) one or more mathematical questions, in Arithmetic, Algebra, or Geometry, as the case might be, for the amusement and possible edification of the fair readers of that Magazine.

"October, 1885.   L. C."

These are regular mathematical problems and "posers," most of them, and it seems that the readers, being more or less ambitious, set to work in right good earnest to answer them, and sent in the solutions to the author under assumed names, and then he produced the real problem, the real answer, and all the best answers of the contestants. These problems were all called*Knots* and were told in the form of stories.

Knot I was called *Excelsior*. It was written as a tale of adventure, and ran as follows:

"The ruddy glow of sunset was already fading into the somber shadows of night, when two travelers might have been observed swiftly—at a pace of six miles in the hour—descending the rugged side of a mountain; the younger bounding from crag to crag with the agility of a fawn, while his companion, whose aged limbs seemed ill at ease in the heavy chain armor habitually worn by tourists in that district, toiled on painfully at his side."

Lewis Carroll is evidently imitating the style of some celebrated writer—Henry James, most likely, who is rather fond of opening his story with "two travelers," or perhaps Sir Walter Scott. He goes on:

"As is always the case under such circumstances, the younger knight was the first to break the silence.

"'A goodly pace, I trow!' he exclaimed. 'We sped not thus in the ascent!'

"'Goodly, indeed!' the other echoed with a groan. 'We clomb it but at three miles in the hour.'

"'And on the dead level our pace is—?' the younger suggested; for he was weak in statistics, and left all such details to his aged companion.

"'Four miles in the hour,' the other wearily replied. 'Not an ounce more,' he added, with that love of metaphor so common in old age, 'and not a farthing less!'

"''Twas three hours past high noon when we left our hostelry,' the young man said, musingly. 'We shall scarce be back by supper-time. Perchance mine host will roundly deny us all food!'

"'He will chide our tardy return,' was the grave reply, 'and such a rebuke will be meet.'

"'A brave conceit!' cried the other, with a merry laugh. 'And should we bid him bring us yet another course, I trow his answer will be tart!'

"'We shall but get our deserts,' sighed the older knight, who had never seen a joke in his life, and was somewhat displeased at his companion's untimely levity. ''Twill be nine of the clock,' he added in an undertone, 'by the time we regain our hostelry. Full many a mile have we plodded this day!'

"'How many? How many?' cried the eager youth, ever athirst for knowledge.

"The old man was silent.

"'Tell me,' he answered after a moment's thought, 'what time it was when we stood together on yonder peak. Not exact to the minute!' he added, hastily, reading a protest in the young man's face. 'An' thy guess be within one poor half hour of the mark, 'tis all I ask of thy mother's son! Then will I tell thee, true to the last inch, how far we shall have trudged betwixt three and nine of the clock.'

"A groan was the young man's only reply, while his convulsed features and the deep wrinkles that chased each other across his manly brow revealed the abyss of arithmetical agony into which one chance question had plunged him."

The problem in plain English is this: "Two travelers spend from three o'clock till nine in walking along a level road, up a hill, and home again, their pace on the level being four miles an hour, up hill three, and down hill six. Find distance walked: also (within half an hour) the time of reaching top of hill."

Answer. "Twenty-four miles: half-past six."

The explanation is very clear and very simple, but we will not give it here. This first knot of "A Tangled Tale" offers attractions of its own, for like the dream *Alice* someone may exclaim, "A Knot! Oh, do let me help to undo it!"

The second problem or "Tale" is called *Eligible Apartments*, and deals with the adventures of one *Balbus* and his pupils, and contains two "Knots." One is: "The Governor of —— wants to give a *very* small dinner party, and he means to ask his father's brother-in-law, his brother's father-in-law, and his brother-in-law's father, and we're to guess how many guests there will be." The answer is *one*. Perhaps some ambitious person will go over the ground and prove it. The second knot deals with the *Eligible Apartments* which *Balbus* and his pupils were hunting. At the end of their walk they found themselves in a square.

"'It *is* a Square!' was Balbus's first cry of delight as he gazed around him. 'Beautiful! Beau-ti-ful! *And* rectangular!' and as he plunged into Geometry he also plunged into funny conversations with the average English landlady, which we can better follow:

"'Which there is *one* room, gentlemen,' said the smiling landlady, 'and a sweet room, too. As snug a little back room——'

"'We will see it,' said Balbus gloomily as they followed her in. 'I knew how it would be! One room in each house! No view I suppose.'

"'Which indeed there *is*, gentlemen!' the landlady indignantly protested as she drew up the blind, and indicated the back garden.

"'Cabbages, I perceive,' said Balbus. 'Well, they're green at any rate.'

"'Which the greens at the shops,' their hostess explained, 'are by no means dependable upon. Here you has them on the premises, *and* of the best.'

"'Does the window open?' was always Balbus's first question in testing a lodging; and 'Does the chimney smoke?' his second. Satisfied on all points, he secured the refusal of the room, and moved on to the next house where they repeated the same performance, adding as an afterthought: 'Does the cat scratch?'

"The landlady looked around suspiciously as if to make sure the cat was not listening. 'I will not deceive you, gentlemen,' she said, 'it *do* scratch, but not without you pulls its whiskers. It'll never do it,' she repeated slowly, with a visible effort to recall the exact words between herself and the cat, 'without you pulls its whiskers!'

"'Much may be excused in a cat so treated,' said Balbus as they left the house, ... leaving the landlady curtseying on the doorstep and still murmuring to herself her parting words, as if they were a form of blessing, 'not without you pulls its whiskers!'"

He has given us a real Dickens atmosphere in the dialogue, but the medicinal problem tucked into it all is too much like hard work.

There were ten of these "Knots," each one harder than its predecessor, and Lewis Carroll found much interest in receiving and criticising the answers, all sent under fictitious names.

This clever mathematician delighted in "puzzlers," and sometimes he found a kindred soul among the guessers, which always pleased him.

One of his favorite problems was one that as early as the days of the *Rectory Umbrella* he brought before his limited public. He called it *Difficulty No. 1*.

"Where in its passage round the earth does the day change its name?"

This question pursued him all through his mathematical career, and the difficulty of answering it has never lessened. Even in "A Tangled Tale" neither Balbus nor his ambitious young pupils could do much with the problem.

Difficulty No. 2 is very humorous, and somewhat of a "catch" question.

"Which is the best—a clock that is right only once a year, or a clock that is right twice every day?"

In March, 1897, *Vanity Fair*, a current English magazine, had the following article entitled:

"A New Puzzle"

"The readers of *Vanity Fair* have, during the last ten years, shown so much interest in Acrostics and Hard Cases, which were at first made the object of sustained competition for prizes in the journal, that it has been sought to invent for them an entirely new kind of Puzzle, such as would interest them equally with those that have already been so successful. The subjoined letter from Mr. Lewis Carroll will explain itself, and will introduce a Puzzle so entirely novel and withal so interesting that the transmutation [changing] of the original into the final word of the Doublets may be expected to become an occupation, to the full as amusing as the guessing of the Double Acrostics has already proved."

"Dear Vanity," Lewis Carroll writes:—"Just a year ago last Christmas two young ladies, smarting under that sorest scourge of feminine humanity, the having "nothing to do," besought me to send them "some riddles." But riddles I had none at hand and therefore set myself to devise some other form of verbal torture which should serve the same purpose. The result of my meditations was a new kind of Puzzle, new at least to me, which now that it has been fairly tested by a year's experience, and commended by many friends, I offer to you as a newly gathered nut to be cracked by the omnivorous teeth that have already masticated so many of your Double Acrostics.

"The rules of the Puzzle are simple enough. Two words are proposed, of the same length; and the Puzzle consists in linking these together by interposing other words, each of which shall differ from the next word *in one letter only*. That is to say, one letter may be changed in one of the given words, then one letter in the word so obtained, and so on, till we arrive at the other given word. The letters must not be interchanged among themselves, but each must keep to its own place. As an example, the word 'head' may be changed into 'tail' by interposing the words 'heal, teal, tell, tall.' I call the two given words 'a Doublet,' the interposed words 'Links,' and the entire series 'a Chain,' of which I here append an example:

Head

heal

teal

tell

tall

Tail

"It is perhaps needless to state that the links should be English words, such as might be used in good society.

"The easiest 'Doublets' are those in which the consonants in one word answer to the consonants in the other, and the vowels to vowels; 'head' and 'tail' constitute a Doublet of this kind. Where this is not the case, as in 'head' and 'hare,' the first thing to be done is to transform one member of the Doublet into a word whose consonants and vowels shall answer to those in the other member ('head, herd, here'), after which there is seldom much difficulty in completing the 'Chain.'...

"LEWIS CARROLL."

"Doublets" was brought out in book form in 1880, and proved a very attractive little volume.

"The Game of Logic" and "A Tangled Tale" are also in book form, the latter cleverly illustrated by Arthur B. Frost.

It would take too long to name all the games and puzzles Lewis Carroll invented. Some were carefully thought out, some were produced on the spur of the moment, generally for the amusement of some special child friend. Indeed, the puzzles and riddles and games had accumulated to such an extent that he was arranging to publish a book of them with illustrations by Miss E. Gertrude Thomson, but after his death the plans fell through, and many literary projects were abandoned.

Acrostic writing was one of his favorite pastimes, and he wrote enough of these to have filled a good fat little volume.

His Wonderland Stamp-Case, one of his own ingenious inventions, might come under the head of "Puzzles and Problems," and, oddly enough, an interesting description of this stamp-case was published only a short time ago in *The Nation*. The writer describes his own copy which he bought when it was new, some twenty years ago. There is first an envelope of red paper, on which is printed:

> The "Wonderland" Postage Stamp-Case,
> Invented by Louis Carroll, Oct. 29, 1888.
> This case contains 12 separate packets for
> Stamps of different values, and 2 Coloured
> Pictorial Surprises, taken from "Alice in
> Wonderland." It is accompanied with 8 or
> 9 Wise Words about Letter-Writing.
>
> 1st, post-free, 13d.

On the flap of the envelope is:

> Published by Emberlin & Son,
> 4 Magdalen Street, Oxford.

"The Stamp-Case," the writer tells us, "consists of a stiff paper folded with the pockets on the inner leaves and a picture on each outer leaf. This Case is inclosed in a sliding cover, and in this way the pictorial surprise becomes possible. A picture of *Alice* holding the *Baby* is on the front cover, and when this is drawn off, there is underneath a picture of *Alice* nursing a pig. On the back cover is the famous *Cat*, which vanishes to a shadowy grin on the pictures beneath."

The booklet which accompanied this little stamp-case found its way to many of his girl friends. Now, whether they bought it, or whether, under guise of giving a present, this clever friend of theirs sent them the stamp-case with the "eight or nine words of advice" slyly tucked in, we cannot say, but in the case of Isa Bowman and of Beatrice Hatch the booklet evidently made a deep impression, for both quote from it very freely, and some of the "wise words" are certainly worth heeding, for instance:

"Address and stamp the envelope."

"What! Before writing the letter?"

"Most certainly; and I'll tell you what will happen if you don't. You will go on writing till the last moment, and just in the middle of the last sentence you will become aware that 'time's up!' Then comes the hurried wind-up—the wildly scrawled signature—the hastily fastened envelope which comes open in the post—the address—a mere hieroglyphic—the horrible discovery that you've forgotten to replenish your stamp-case—the frantic appeal to everyone in the house to lend you a stamp—the headlong rush to the Post Office, arriving hot and gasping, just after the box has been closed—and finally, a week afterwards, the return of the letter from the dead letter office, marked, 'address illegible.'"

"Write legibly.

"The average temper of the human race would be perceptibly sweetened if everybody obeyed this rule. A great deal of bad writing in the world comes simply from writing *too quickly*. Of course you reply, 'I do it to save time.' A very good object no doubt; but what right have you to do it at your friend's expense? Isn't his time as valuable as yours? Years ago I used to receive letters from a friend—and very interesting letters too—written in one of the most atrocious hands ever invented. It generally took me about a week to read one of his letters! I used to carry it about in my pocket and take it out at leisure times to puzzle over the riddles which composed it—holding it in different positions, till at last the meaning of some hopeless scrawl would flash upon me, when I at once wrote down the English under it; and when several had thus been guessed, the context would help me with the others till at last the whole series of hieroglyphics was deciphered. If all one's friends wrote like that, life would be entirely spent in reading their letters!"

"*My Ninth Rule.*—When you get to the end of a note-sheet, and find you have more to say, take another piece of paper—a whole sheet or a scrap, as the case may demand, but whatever you do, *don't cross*! Remember the old proverb 'Cross-writing makes cross-reading.' 'The *old* proverb?' you say inquiringly. 'How old?' Why, not so *very* ancient, I must confess. In fact—I'm afraid I invented it while writing this paragraph. Still, you know 'old' is a *comparative* term; I think you would be quite justified in addressing a chicken just out of the shell as 'Old Boy!' *when compared* with another chicken that was only half out!"

"Don't try to have the last word," he tells us—and again, "*Don't* fill more than a page and a half with apologies for not having written sooner."

"*On how to end a letter*," he advises the writer to "refer to your correspondent's last letter, and make your winding up *at least as friendly as his*; in fact, even if a shade more friendly, it will do no harm."

"When you take your letters to the post, *carry them in your hand*. If you put them in your pocket, you will take a long country walk (I speak from experience), passing the post office twice, going and returning, and when you get home you will find them still in your pocket."

Letter-writing was as much a part of Lewis Carroll as games, and puzzles, and problems, and mathematics, and nonsense, and little girls. Indeed, as we view him through the stretch of years, we find him so many-sided that he himself would have done well to draw a new geometrical figure to represent a nature so full of strange angles and surprising shapes. If one is fond of looking into a kaleidoscope, and watching the ever-changing facets and colors and designs, one would be pretty apt to understand the constant shifting of that active mind, always on the alert for new ideas, but steady and fixed in many good old ones, which had become firm habits.

He was fond of giving his child-friends "nuts to crack," and nothing pleased him more than to be the center of some group of little girls, firing his conundrums and puzzles into their minds, and watching the bright young faces catching the glow of his thoughts. He knew just how far to go, and when to turn some dawning idea into quaint nonsense, so that the young mind could grasp and hold it. Dear maker of nonsense, dear teacher and friend, dear lover of children, can they ever forget you!

Chapter XII

A Fairy Ring of Girls

In a little poem called "A Sea Dirge," which Lewis Carroll wrote about this time, we find some very strange, uncomplimentary remarks, considering the fact that most of his vacations was spent at the seashore. Eastbourne, in the summer time, was as much his home—during the last fifteen years of his life—as Christ Church during the Oxford term. His pretty house in a shady, quiet street was a familiar spot to every girl friend of his acquaintance, and many of his closest and most interesting friendships were begun by the sea, yet he says:

> There are certain things, as a spider, a ghost,
>   The income-tax, gout, an umbrella for three—
> That I hate, but the thing that I hate the most
>   Is a thing they call the Sea.
>
> Pour some salt water over the floor—
>   Ugly I'm sure you'll allow it to be;
> Suppose it extended a mile or more,
>   *That's* very like the Sea.
>
> . . . .
>
> I had a vision of nursery maids;
>   Tens of thousands passed by me—
> All leading children with wooden spades,
>   And this way by the Sea.
>
> Who invented those spades of wood?
>   Who was it cut them out of the tree?
> None, I think, but an idiot could—
>   Or one that loved the Sea.
>
> . . . .

> If you like your coffee with sand for dregs,
>   A decided hint of salt in your tea,
> And a fishy taste in the very eggs—
>   By all means choose the Sea.
>
> And if, with these dainties to drink and eat,
>   You prefer not a vestige of grass or tree,
> And a chronic state of wet in your feet,
>   Then—I recommend the Sea.

Did he mean all this, we wonder, this genial gentleman, who haunted the seashore in search of little girls, his pockets bulging with games and puzzles? He had also a good supply of safety-pins, in case he saw someone who wanted to wade in the sea, but whose skirts were in her way and who had no pin handy. Then he would go gravely up to her and present her with one of his stock.

In the earlier days he used to go to Sandown, in the Isle of Wight, and there he met little Gertrude Chataway, who must have been a very charming child, for he promptly fell in love with her. This was in 1875, and, from her description of him, he must have been a *very, very* old gentleman—forty-three at least. He happened to live next door to Gertrude, and during those summer days she used to watch him with much interest, for he had a way of throwing back his head and sniffing in the salt air that fascinated Gertrude, whose joy bubbled over when at last he spoke to her. The two became great friends. They used to sit for hours on the steps of their house which led to the beach, and he would delight the little girl with his wonderful stories, often illustrating them with a pencil as he talked. The great charm of these stories lay in the fact that some chance remark of Gertrude's would wind him up; some question she asked would suggest a story, and as it spread out into "lovely nonsense" she always felt in some way that she had helped to make it grow.

This little girl was one of the child-friends who clung to the sweet association all her life, just as the little Liddell girls never grew quite away from his love and interest. It was to Gertrude that he dedicated "The Hunting of the Snark," and she was the proud possessor not only of his friendship, but of many interesting letters, covering a period of at least ten years, during which time Gertrude passed from little girlhood, though he never seemed to realize the change.

Two of his prime favorites in the earlier days were Ellen Terry, the well-known English actress, and her sister Kate, who was also an actress of some note.

Lewis Carroll, being always very fond of the drama, found it through life his keenest delight, and it was his good fortune to see little Ellen Terry in the first prominent part she ever took. This was in 1856, when Mr. and Mrs. Charles Kean played in "The Winter's Tale," and Ellen took the child's character of *Mamillius*, the little son of the King. Lewis Carroll was carried away with the tiny actress, and it did not take him long after that to make her acquaintance. This no doubt began in the usual way, a chat with the child behind the scenes, a call upon her father and mother, and, finally, an introduction to the whole family which, being nearly as large as his own, could not fail to interest him deeply.

There were two other little Terry girls, who attracted him and to whom he was very kind, Florence and Marion. The boys, and there were five of them, he never noticed of course, but the four little girls came in for a good share of the most substantial petting. Many a day at the seaside he gave them—these busy little actresses—many a feast in his own rooms, many a daytime frolic, for night was their working time—not that they minded in the least, for they loved their work. There was much talk in those days about the harm in allowing children to act at night, when they should be snug in their beds dreaming of fairies. But Lewis Carroll thought nothing of the kind; he delighted in the children's acting, and he knew, being half a child himself, that the youngsters took as much delight in their work as he did in seeing them. He always contended that acting comes naturally to children; from babyhood they "pretend," and if they happen, as in Ellen Terry's case and the case of other little stage people he knew, to be born in the profession, why, this "pretending" is the finest kind of *play* not *work*. So he was always on the side of the little actors and actresses who did not want to be taken away from the theater and put to bed.

Ellen Terry proved also to be one of his lifelong friends; the talented actress found his praise a most precious thing, and his criticism, always so honest, and usually so keen and true, she accepted with the grace of the great artist. Often, too, he asked her aid for some other girl friend with dramatic talent, and she never failed to lend a helping hand when she could. From first to last her acting charmed him. Often he would take a little girl to some Shakespearean treat at the theater, and would raise her to the "seventh heaven" of delight by penciling a note to Miss Terry asking for an interview or perhaps a photograph for his small companion, and these requests were never refused.

Every Christmas the Rev. Charles Dodgson spent with his sisters, who since their father's death had lived at Guildford, in a pretty house called *The Chestnuts*. His coming at Christmas was always a great event, for of course some very youthful ladies in the neighborhood were in a state of suppressed excitement over his yearly arrival, which meant Christmas jollity—with charades and tableaux and all sorts of odd and interesting games, and, *of course*, stories.

One of his special Guildford favorites was Gaynor Simpson, to whom he wrote several of his clever letters. In one, evidently an answer to hers, he begged her never again to leave out the g in the name Dodgson, asking in a very plaintive manner what *she* would think if he left out the G in *her* name and called her "Aynor" instead of Gaynor.

In this same letter he confessed that he never danced except in his own peculiar way, that the last house he danced in, the floors broke through, but as the beams were only six inches thick, it was a very poor sort of floor, when one came to think—that stone arches were much better for *his* sort of dancing.

Indeed, the poem he wrote about the sea must have been just a bit of a joke, for it was at Margate, another seaside resort, that he met Adelaide Paine, another of his favorites, and to her he presented a copy of "The Hunting of the Snark," with an acrostic on her name written on the fly leaf. This little maid was further honored by receiving a photograph, not of Lewis Carroll, but of Mr. Dodgson, and in a note to her mother he begged in his usual odd way that she would never let any but her intimate friends know anything about the name of "Lewis Carroll," as he did not wish people who had heard of him to recognize him in the street.

The friendships that were not cemented at the seaside or under the shelter of old "Tom Quad" were very often begun in the railway train. English trains are not like ours in America. In Lewis Carroll's time the "first-class" accommodations were called *carriages*, in which four or five people, often total strangers, were shut up for hours together, actually locked in by the guard; and if one of these people chanced to be Lewis Carroll, and another a restless, active little girl, why, in the twinkling of an eye the sign of fellowship had flashed between them, and they were friends.

One special friend made in this fashion was a dear little maid named Kathleen Eschwege, who stayed a child to him always during their eighteen years of friendship, in spite of all the changes the years brought in their train, her marriage among the rest, on which occasion he wrote her that as he never gave wedding presents, he hoped the inclosed he sent in his letter she would accept as an *unwedding* present.

This letter bore the date of January 20, 1892; five years later he wrote to acknowledge a photograph she had sent him in January, 1892, also her wedding-card in August of the same year. But he salved his conscience by reminding her that a certain biscuit-box— decorated with "Looking-Glass" pictures—which he had sent her in December, 1892, had never been acknowledged by *her*.

Our "don's" memory sometimes played him tricks we see, especially in later years. On one occasion, failing to recognize someone who passed him on the street, he was much chagrined to find out that he had been the gentleman's guest at dinner only the night before.

Another pleasant railway friendship was established with three little Drury girls, as early as 1869. They did not know who he was until he sent them a copy of "Alice in Wonderland"—with the following verse on the fly leaf:

TO THREE PUZZLED LITTLE GIRLS

(*From the Author.*)

Three little maidens weary of the rail,
Three pairs of little ears listening to a tale,
Three little hands held out in readiness
For three little puzzles very hard to guess.
Three pairs of little eyes and open wonder-wide
At three little scissors lying side by side,
Three little mouths that thanked an unknown friend
For one little book he undertook to send.
Though whether they'll remember a friend or book or
day—
In three little weeks is very hard to say.

Edith Rix was another favorite but apparently beyond the usual age, for his letters to her have quite a grown-up tone, and he helped her through many girlish quandaries with his wholesome advice.

There are scores of others—so many that their very names would mean nothing to us unless we knew the circumstances which began the acquaintance, and the numerous incidents which could only occur in the company of Lewis Carroll.

As we know, there were three great influences in his life: his reverence for holy things, his fondness for mathematics, and his love of little girls. It is this last trait which colors our picture of him and makes him stand forth in our minds apart from other men of his time. There have been many great preachers and eminent mathematicians, and these brilliant men may have loved childhood in a certain way, but to step aside from their high places to mingle with the children would never have occurred to them. The small girls who were "seen and not heard" dropped their eyes bashfully when the great ones passed, and bobbed a little old-fashioned curtsy in return for a stately preoccupied nod. But not so Lewis Carroll. No childish eyes ever sought his in vain. His own blue ones always smiled back, and there was something so glowing in this smile which lit up his whole face, that children, all unconsciously, drew near the warmth of it.

His love for girls speaks well for the home-life and surroundings of his earlier years, when in the company of his seven sisters he learned to know girls pretty thoroughly. These girls of whom we have such scant knowledge possessed, we are sure, some potent charm to make this "big brother" forever afterwards the champion of little girls, and being a thoughtful fellow, he must have watched with pleasure the way they bloomed from childhood to girlhood and from girlhood to womanhood, in the sweet seclusion of Croft Rectory. It was this intimacy and comradeship with his sisters which made him so easily the intimate and comrade of so many little girls, understanding all their traits and peculiarities and their "girl nature" better sometimes than they did themselves.

Some of his friends moved in royal circles. Princess Beatrice, who received the second presentation copy of "Alice in Wonderland," was one of them; but in later years the two children of the Duchess of Albany (Queen Victoria's daughter-in-law), Alice and the young Duke, claimed his friendship, and despite his preference for girls, Lewis Carroll could not help liking the lad, whose gentle disposition and studious habits set him somewhat apart from other boys.

Near home, that is to say in Oxford, or more properly, within a stone's throw of Christ Church itself, dwelt the Rev. E. Hatch and his bright and interesting family of children, with all of whom Lewis Carroll was on the most intimate terms, though his special favorite was Beatrice, better known as Bee. This little girl came so close upon the Liddell children in his long list of friends that she almost caught the echo of those happy days of "Wonderland," and she has much to say about this association in an interesting article published in the *Strand Magazine* some years ago.

"My earliest recollections of Mr. Dodgson," she writes, "are connected with photography. He was very fond of this art at one time, though he had entirely given it up for many years latterly. He kept various costumes and 'properties' with which to dress us up, and of course that added to the fun. What child would not thoroughly enjoy personating a Japanese or a beggar child or a gypsy or an Indian? Sometimes there were excursions to the roof of the college, which was easily accessible from the windows of the studio. Or you might stand by your tall friend's side in the tiny dark room, and watch him while he poured the contents of several little strong-smelling bottles on the glass picture of yourself that looked so funny with its black face; and when you grew tired of this there were many delights to be found in the cupboards in the big room downstairs. Musical boxes of different colors and different tunes, the dear old woolly bear that walked when he was wound up, toys, picture-books, and packets of photographs of other children, who had also enjoyed these mornings of bliss.

"The following letter written to me in 1873, about a large wax doll that Mr. Dodgson had presented to me, and which I left behind when I went on a visit from home, is an interesting specimen. Emily and Mabel [referred to in the letter] were other dolls of mine and known also by him, but though they have long since departed this life, I need hardly say I still possess*the* doll 'Alice.'

"'My dear Birdie: I met her just outside Tom Gate, walking very stiffly and I think she was trying to find her way to my rooms. So I said, "Why have you come here without Birdie?" So she said, "Birdie's gone! and Emily's gone! and Mabel isn't kind to me!"' And two little waxy tears came running down her cheeks.

"Why, how stupid of me! I've never told who it was all the time! It was your own doll. I was very glad to see her, and took her to my room, and gave her some Vesta matches to eat, and a cup of nice melted wax to drink, for the poor little thing was very hungry and thirsty after her long walk. So I said, 'Come and sit by the fire and let's have a comfortable chat?' 'Oh, no! no!' she said, 'I'd *much* rather not; you know I do melt so *very* easily!' And she made me take her quite to the other side of the room, where it was *very* cold; and then she sat on my knee and fanned herself with a pen-wiper, because she said she was afraid the end of her nose was beginning to melt.

"'You have no *idea* how careful we have to be—we dolls,' she said. 'Why, there was a sister of mine—would you believe it?—she went up to the fire to warm her hands, and one of her hands dropped right off! There now!' 'Of course it dropped *right* off,' I said, 'because it was the *right* hand.' 'And how do you know it was the *right* hand, Mister Carroll?' the doll said. So I said, 'I think it must have been the *right* hand because the other hand was *left*.'

"The doll said, 'I shan't laugh. It's a very bad joke. Why, even a common wooden doll could make a better joke than that. And besides they've made my mouth so stiff and hard that I *can't* laugh if I try ever so much.' 'Don't be cross about it,' I said, 'but tell me this: I'm going to give Birdie and the other children one photograph each, whichever they choose; which do you think Birdie will choose?' 'I don't know,' said the doll; 'you'd better ask her!' So I took her home in a hansom cab. Which would you like, do you think? Arthur as Cupid? or Arthur and Wilfred together? or you and Ethel as beggar children? or Ethel standing on a box? or, one of yourself?

"'Your affectionate friend,
"'LEWIS CARROLL.'"

There were, as you see, special occasions when boys were accepted, or rather tolerated, and special boys with whom he exchanged courtesies from time to time. The little Hatch boys were favored, we cannot say for their own small sakes, but because there were two little sisters and *their* feelings had to be considered. Lewis Carroll even took their pictures, and went so far as to write a little prologue for Beatrice and her brother Wilfred. The "grownups" were to give some private theatricals which the children were to introduce in the following dialogue:

(Enter Beatrice leading Wilfred. She leaves him at center [front], and after going round on tiptoe to make sure they are not overheard, returns and takes his arm.)

B. Wiffie! I'm *sure* that something is the matter!
   All day there's been-oh, such a fuss and clatter!
   Mamma's been trying on a funny dress—
   I never saw the house in such a mess!
                         (*Puts her arms around his neck.*)
   Is there a secret, Wiffie?

W. (*Shaking her off.*) Yes, of course!

B. And you won't tell it? (*Whimpers*) Then you're very
   cross!
   (*Turns away from him and clasps her hands ecstatically.*)
   I'm sure of this! It's something *quite* uncommon!

W. (*Stretching up his arms with a mock heroic air.*)
   Oh, Curiosity! Thy name is woman!
                         (*Puts his arm round her coaxingly.*)
   Well, Birdie, then I'll tell! (*Mysteriously.*)
   What should you say
   If they were going to act—a little play?

B. (*Jumping up and clapping her hands.*)
   I'd say, "How nice!"

W. (*Pointing to audience.*)
   But will it please the rest?

B. Oh, yes! Because, you know, they'll do their best!
                         (*Turns to audience.*)
   You'll praise them, won't you, when you've seen the play?
   Just say, "How nice!" before you go away!
                         (*They run away hand in hand.*)

Of course the little girl had the last word, but then, as Lewis
Carroll himself would say, "Little girls usually had."

This prologue, Miss Hatch tells us, was Lewis Carroll's only
attempt in the dramatic line, and the two tots made a pretty picture
as they ran off the stage.

"Mr. Dodgson's chief form of entertaining," writes Miss Hatch, "was giving dinner parties. Do not misunderstand me, nor picture to yourself a long row of guests on either side of a gayly-decorated table. Mr. Dodgson's theory was that it was much more enjoyable to have your friends singly, consequently these 'dinner parties,' as he liked to call them, consisted almost always of one guest only, and that one a child friend. One of his charming and characteristic little notes, written in his clear writing, often on a half sheet of note paper and signed with the C.L.D. monogram 🔄 would arrive, containing an invitation, of which the following is a specimen." [Though written when Beatrice was no longer a little girl.]

Ch. Ch. Nov. 21, '96.

"'MY DEAR BEE:—The reason I have for so long a time not visited the hive is a *logical* one," (he was busy on his symbolic *Logic*), "'but is not (as you might imagine) that I think there is no more honey in it! Will you come and dine with me? Any day would suit me, and I would fetch you at 6:30.

"Ever your affectionate
"'C.L.D.'

"Let us suppose this invitation has been accepted.... After turning in at the door of No. 7 staircase, and mounting a rather steep and winding stair, we find ourselves outside a heavy black door, of somewhat prisonlike appearance, over which is painted 'The Rev. C. L. Dodgson.' Then a passage, then a door with glass panels, and at last we reach the familiar room that we love so well. It is large and lofty and extremely cheerful-looking. All around the walls are bookcases and under them the cupboards of which I have spoken, and which even now we long to see opened that they may pour out their treasures.

"Opposite to the big window with its cushioned seat is the fireplace; and this is worthy of some notice on account of the lovely red tiles which represent the story of 'The Hunting of the Snark.' Over the mantelpiece hang three painted portraits of child friends, the one in the middle being the picture of a little girl in a blue cap and coat who is carrying a pair of skates."

This picture is a fine likeness of Xie (Alexandra) Kitchin, the little daughter of the Dean of Durham, another of his Oxford favorites.

"Mr. Dodgson," continues Miss Hatch, "seats his guest in a corner of the red sofa, in front of the fireplace, and the few minutes before dinner are occupied with anecdotes about other child friends, small or grown up, or anything in particular that has happened to himself.... Dinner is served in the smaller room, which is also filled with bookcases and books.... Those who have had the privilege of enjoying a college dinner need not be told how excellent it is.... The rest of the evening slips away very quickly, there is so much to be shown. You may play a game—one of Mr. Dodgson's own invention— ... or you may see pictures, lovely drawings of fairies, whom your host tells you 'you can't be sure don't really exist.' Or you may have music if you wish it."

This was of course before the days of the phonograph, but Lewis Carroll had the next best thing, which Miss Hatch describes as an organette, in a large square box, through the side of which a handle is affixed. "Another box holds the tunes, circular perforated cards, all carefully catalogued by their owner. The picture of the author of 'Alice' keenly enjoying every note as he solemnly turns the handle, and raises or closes the lid of the box to vary the sound, is more worthy of your delight than the music itself. Never was there a more delightful host for a 'dinner-party' or one who took such pains for your entertainment, fresh and interesting to the last."

One of the first things a little girl learned in her intercourse with Lewis Carroll was to be methodical and orderly, as he was himself, in the arrangement of papers, photographs, and books; he kept lists and registers of everything. Miss Hatch tells of a wonderful letter register of his own invention "that not only recorded the names of his correspondents and the dates of their letters, but also noted the contents of each communication, so that in a few seconds he could tell you what you had written to him about on a certain day in years gone by.

"Another register contained a list of every menu supplied to every guest who dined at Mr. Dodgson's table. Yet," she explains, "his dinners were simple enough, never more than two courses. But everything that he did must be done in the most perfect manner possible, and the same care and attention would be given to other people's affairs, if in any way he could assist or give them pleasure.

"If he took you up to London to see a play, you were no sooner seated in the railway carriage than a game was produced from his bag and all the occupants were invited to join in playing a kind of 'Halma' or 'draughts' of his own invention, on the little wooden board that had been specially made at his design for railway use, with 'men' warranted not to tumble down, because they fitted into little holes in the board."

Children, little girls especially, remember through life the numberless small kindnesses that are shown to them. Is it any wonder, then, that the name of Lewis Carroll is held in such loving memory by the scores of little girls he drew about him? Beatrice Hatch was only one among many to feel the warmth of his love. This quiet, almost solitary, man whose home was in the shadow of a great college, whose daily life was such a long walk of dull routine, could yet find time to make his own sunshine and to draw others into the light of it.

But the children did *their* part too. He grew dependent on them as the years rolled on; a fairy circle of girls was always drawing him to them, and he was made one of them. They told him their childish secrets feeling sure of a ready sympathy and a quick appreciation. He seemed to know his way instinctively to a girl's heart; she felt for him an affection, half of comradeship, half of reverence, for there was something inspiring in the fearless carriage of the head, the clear, serene look in the eyes, that seemed to pierce far ahead upon the path over which their own young feet were stumbling, perhaps.

With the passing of the years, some of the seven sisters married, and a fair crop of nieces and nephews shot up around him, also some small cousins in whom he took a deep interest. It is to one of these that he dedicated his poem called "Matilda Jane," in honor of the doll who bore the name, which meant nothing in the world to such an unresponsive bit of doll-dom.

Matilda Jane, you never look
At any toy or picture book;
I show you pretty things in vain,
You must be blind, Matilda Jane!

I ask you riddles, tell you tales,
But all our conversation fails;
You never answer me again,
I fear you're dumb, Matilda Jane!

Matilda, darling, when I call,
You never seem to hear at all;
I shout with all my might and main,
But you're *so* deaf, Matilda Jane!

Matilda Jane, you needn't mind,
For though you're deaf and dumb and blind,
There's some one loves you, it is plain,
And that is *me*, Matilda Jane!

A little tender-hearted, ungrammatical, motherly *"me"*—how well the writer knew the small "Bessie" whose affection for this doll inspired the verses!

In after years when more serious work held him close to his study, and he made a point of declining all invitations, he took care that no small girl should be put on his black list. "If," says Miss Hatch, "you were very anxious to get him to come to your house on any particular day, the only chance was *not* to *invite* him, but only to inform him that you would be at home; otherwise he would say 'As you have *invited* me, I cannot come, for I have made a rule to decline all *invitations*, but I will come the next day,'" and in answer to an invitation to tea, he wrote her in his whimsical way:

"What an awful proposition! To drink tea from four to six would tax the constitution even of a hardened tea-drinker. For me, who hardly ever touches it, it would probably be fatal."

If only we could read half the clever letters which passed between Lewis Carroll and his girl friends, what a volume of wit and humor, of sound common sense, of clever nonsense we should find! Yet behind it all, that underlying seriousness which made his friendship so precious to those who were so fortunate as to possess it. The "little girl" whose loving picture of him tells us so much lived near him all her life; she felt his influence in all the little things that go to make up a child's day, long after the real childhood had passed her by. And so with all the girls who knew and loved him, and even those to whom his name was but a suggestion of what he really was.

Surely this fairy ring of girls encircles the English-speaking world, the girls whom Lewis Carroll loved, the hundreds he knew, the millions he had never seen.

Chapter XIII

'Alice' on the Stage and Off

Then the question of dramatizing the "Alice" books was placed before the author, by Mr. Savile Clarke, who was to undertake the work, he consented gladly enough. It was to be an operetta of two acts; the libretto, or story part, by Mr. Clarke himself, the music by Mr. Walter Slaughter, and the only condition Lewis Carroll made was that nothing should be written or acted which should in any way be unsuitable for children.

Of course, everything was done under his eye, and he wrote an extra song for the ghosts of the *Oysters*, who had been eaten by the *Walrus* and the *Carpenter*; he also finished that poetic gem, "'Tis the Voice of the Lobster."

"'Tis the voice of the Lobster," I heard him declare,
"You baked me too brown, I must sugar my hair."
As a duck with its eyelids, so he with his nose,
Trims his belt and his buttons, and turns out his toes.
When the sands are all dry, he is gay as a lark
And talks with the utmost contempt of a shark;
But when the tide rises and sharks are around,
His words have a timid and tremulous sound.

I passed by his garden, and marked with one eye
How the Owl and the Panther were sharing a pie:
The Panther took pie, crust and gravy and meat,
While the Owl had the dish, for his share of the treat.
When the pie was all finished, the Owl—as a boon
Was kindly permitted to pocket the spoon;
While the Panther received knife and fork with a growl,
And concluded the banquet——

That is how the poem originally ended, but musically that would never do, so the last two lines were altered in this fashion:

> "But the Panther obtained both the fork and the knife,
> So when he lost his temper, the Owl lost his life,"

and a rousing little song it made.

The play was produced at the Prince of Wales' Theater, during Christmas week of 1886, where it was a great success. Lewis Carroll himself specially praises the Wonderland act, notably the Mad Tea Party. The *Hatter* was finely done by Mr. Sidney Harcourt, the *Dormouse* by little Dorothy d'Alcourt, aged six-and-a-half, and Phœbe Carlo, he tells us, was a "splendid *Alice.*"

He went many times to see his "dream child" on the stage, and was always very kind to the little actresses, whose dainty work made *his* work such a success. Phœbe Carlo became a very privileged young person and enjoyed many treats of his giving, to say nothing of a personal gift of a copy of "Alice" from the delighted author.

After the London season, the play was taken through the English provinces and was much appreciated wherever it went. On one occasion a company gave a week's performance at Brighton, and Lewis Carroll happening to be there one afternoon, came across three of the small actresses down on the beach and spent several hours with them. "Happy, healthy little girls" he called them, and no doubt that beautiful afternoon they had the time of their lives.

These children, he found—and he had made the subject quite a study—had been acting every day in the week, and twice on the day before he met them, and yet were energetic enough to get up each morning at seven for a sea bath, to run races on the pier, and to be quite ready for another performance that night.

On December 26, 1888, there was an elaborate revival of "Alice" at the Royal Globe Theater. In the *London Times* the next morning appeared this notice:

> "'Alice in Wonderland,' having failed to exhaust its popularity at the Prince of Wales' Theater, has been revived at the Globe for

a series of matinées during the holiday season. Many members of the old cast remain in the bill, but a new 'Alice' is presented in Miss Isa Bowman, who is not only a wonderful actress for her years, but also a nimble dancer.

"In its new surroundings the fantastic scenes of the story—so cleverly transferred from the book to the stage by Mr. Savile Clarke—lose nothing of their original brightness and humor. 'Alice's Adventures in Wonderland and Through the Looking-Glass' have the rare charm of freshness for children and for their elders, and the many strange personages concerned—the White Rabbit, the Caterpillar, the Cheshire Cat, the Hatter, the Dormouse, the Gryphon, the Mock Turtle, the Red and White Kings and Queens, the Walrus, Humpty-Dumpty, Tweedledum and Tweedledee, and all the rest of them—being seen at home, so to speak, and not on parade as in an ordinary pantomime. Even the dreaded Jabberwock pays an unconventional visit to the company from the 'flies,' and his appearance will not be readily forgotten. As before, Mr. Walter Slaughter's music is an agreeable element to the performance...."

The programme of this performance certainly spreads a feast before the children's eyes. First of all, think of a forest in autumn! (They had to change the season a little to get the bright colors of red and yellow.) Here it is that *Alice* falls asleep and the Elves sing to her. Then there is the awakening in Wonderland—such a Wonderland as few children dreamed of. And then all our favorites appear and do just the things we always thought they would do if they had the chance. The *Cheshire Cat* grins and vanishes, and then the grin appears without the cat, and then the cat grows behind the grin, and everything is so impossible and wonderful that one shivers with delight. There is a good old fairy tale that every child knows; it is called "Oh! if I could but shiver!" and everyone who really enjoys a fairy tale understands the feeling—the delight of shivering—to see the Jabberwock pass before you in all his terrifying, delicious ugliness, flapping his huge wings, rolling his bulging eyes, and opening and shutting those dreadful jaws of his; and yet to know he isn't "*really, real*" any more than Sir John Tenniel's picture of him in the dear old "Alice" book at home, that you can actually go with *Alice* straight into Wonderland and back again, safe and sound, and really see what happened just as she did, and actually squeeze through into Looking-Glass Land, all made so delightfully possible by clever scenery and acting.

A more charming, dainty little "Alice" never danced herself into the heart of anyone as Isa Bowman did into the heart of Lewis Carroll. She came into his life when all of his best-beloved children had passed forever beyond the portals of childhood, never to return; loved more in these later days for the memory of what they had been. But here was a child who aroused all the associations of earlier years, who had made "Alice" real again, whose clever acting gave just that dreamlike, elfin touch which the real Alice of Long Ago had suggested; a sweet-natured, lovable, most attractive child, the child perhaps who won his deepest affections because she came to him when the others had vanished, and clung to him in the twilight.

There must have been several little Bowmans. We know of four little sisters—Isa, Emsie, Nellie, and Maggie, and Master Charles Bowman was the *Cheshire Cat* in the revival of "Alice in Wonderland," and to all of these—we are considering the girls of course, the boy never counted—Lewis Carroll showed his sweetest, most lovable side. They called him "Uncle," and a more devoted uncle they could not possibly have found. As for Isa herself, there was a special niche all her own; she was, as he often told her, "*his* little girl," and in a loving memoir of him she has given to the world of children a beautiful picture of what he really was.

There was something in the grip of his firm white hands, in his glance so deeply sympathetic, so tender and kind, that always stirred the little girl just as her sharp eyes noted a certain peculiarity in his walk. His stammer also impressed her, for it generally came when he least expected it, and though he tried all his life to cure it, he never succeeded.

His shyness, too, was very noticeable, not so much with children, except just at first until he knew them well, but with grown people he was, as she put it, "almost old-maidishly prim in his manner." This shyness was shown in many ways, particularly in a morbid horror of having his picture taken. As fond as he was of taking other people, he dreaded seeing his own photograph among strangers, and once when Isa herself made a caricature of him, he suddenly got up from his seat, took the drawing out of her hands, tore it in small pieces and threw it into the fire without a word; then he caught the frightened little girl in his strong arms and kissed her passionately, his face, at first so flushed and angry, softening with a tender light.

Many and many a happy time she spent with him at Oxford. He found rooms for her just outside the college gates, and a nice comfortable dame to take charge of her. The long happy days were spent in his rooms, and every night at nine she was taken over to the little house in St. Aldates ("St. Olds") and put to bed by the landlady.

In the morning the deep notes of "Great Tom" woke her and then began another lovely day with her "Uncle." She speaks of two tiny turret rooms, one on each side of his staircase in Christ Church. "He used to tell me," she writes, "that when I grew up and became married, he would give me the two little rooms, so that if I ever disagreed with my husband, we could each of us retire to a turret until we had made up our quarrel."

She, too, was fascinated by his collection of music-boxes, the finest, she thought, to be found anywhere in the world. "There were big black ebony boxes with glass tops, through which you could see all the works. There was a big box with a handle, which it was quite hard exercise for a little girl to turn, and there must have been twenty or thirty little ones which could only play one tune. Sometimes one of the musical boxes would not play properly and then I always got tremendously excited. Uncle used to go to a drawer in the table and produce a box of little screw-drivers and punches, and while I sat on his knee, he would unscrew the lid and take out the wheels to see what was the matter. He must have been a clever mechanist, for the result was always the same—after a longer or shorter period, the music began again. Sometimes, when the musical boxes had played all their tunes, he used to put them in the box backwards, and was as pleased as I was at the comic effect of the music 'standing on its head,' as he phrased it.

"There was another and very wonderful toy which he sometimes produced for me, and this was known as 'The Bat.' The ceilings of the rooms in which he lived were very high, indeed, and admirably suited for the purposes of 'The Bat.' It was an ingeniously constructed toy of gauze and wire, which actually flew about the room like a bat. It was worked by a piece of twisted elastic, and it could fly for about half a minute. I was always a little afraid of this toy because it was too lifelike, but there was a fearful joy in it. When the music boxes began to pall, he would get up from his chair and look at me with a knowing smile. I always knew what was coming, even before he began to speak, and I used to dance up and down in tremendous anticipation.

"'Isa, my darling,' he would say, 'once upon a time there was someone called Bob, the Bat! and he lived in the top left-hand drawer of the writing table. What could he do when Uncle wound him up?'"

"And then I would squeak out breathlessly: 'He could really fly!'"

And Bob the Bat had many wonderful adventures. She tells us how, on a hot summer morning when the window was wide open, Bob flew out into the garden and landed in a bowl of salad that one of the servants was carrying to someone's room. The poor fellow was so frightened by this sudden apparition that he promptly dropped the bowl, breaking it into countless pieces.

Lewis Carroll never liked "his little girl" to exaggerate. "I remember," she tells us, "how annoyed he once was when, after a morning's sea bathing at Eastbourne, I exclaimed: 'Oh, this salt water, it always makes my hair as stiff as a poker!'

"He impressed upon me quite irritably that no little girl's hair could ever possibly get as *stiff as a poker*. 'If you had said "as stiff as wires" it would have been more like it, but even that would have been an exaggeration.' And then seeing I was a little frightened, he drew for me a picture of 'The little girl called Isa, whose hair turned into pokers because she was always exaggerating things.'

"'I nearly died of laughing' was another expression that he particularly disliked; in fact, any form of exaggeration generally called from him a reproof, though he was sometimes content to make fun. For instance, my sisters and I had sent him 'millions of kisses' in a letter.' Here is his answer:

"'Ch. Ch. Oxford. Ap. 14, 1890.

"'MY OWN DARLING:

"'It's all very well for you and Nellie and Emsie to write in millions of hugs and kisses, but please consider the *time* it would occupy your poor old very busy uncle! Try hugging and kissing Emsie for a minute by the watch and I don't think you'll manage it more than 20 times a minute. "Millions" must mean two millions at least.'"

Then follows a characteristic example in arithmetic:

20)2,000,000 hugs and kisses.

60)100,000 minutes.

12)1,666 hours.

6)138 days (at twelve hours a day).

23 weeks.

"I couldn't go on hugging and kissing more than 12 hours a day; and I wouldn't like to spend *Sundays* that way. So you see it would take 23 weeks of hard work. Really, my dear child, I cannot spare the time.

"Why haven't I written since my last letter? Why, how could I have written *since the last time I did* write? Now you just try it with kissing. Go and kiss Nellie, from me, several times, and take care to manage it so as to have kissed her *since the last time you did* kiss her. Now go back to your place and I'll question you.

"'Have you kissed her several times?'

"'Yes, darling Uncle.'

"'What o'clock was it when you gave her the *last* kiss?'

"'Five minutes past 10, Uncle.'

"'Very well, now, have you kissed her *since*?'

"'Well—I—ahem! ahem! ahem! (excuse me, Uncle, I've got a bad cough) I—think—that—I—that is, you know, I—'

"'Yes, I see! "Isa" begins with "I," and it seems to me as if she was going to *end* with "I" *this* time!'"

The rest of the letter refers to Isa's visit to America, when she went to play the little *Duke of York* in "Richard III."

"Mind you don't write me from there," he warns her. "Please, *please*, no more horrid letters from you! I *do* hate them so! And as for kissing them when I get them, why, I'd just as soon kiss—kiss—kiss—*you*, you tiresome thing! So there now!

"Thank you very much for those 2 photographs—I liked them—hum—*pretty* well. I can't honestly say I thought them the very best I had ever seen.

"Please give my kindest regards to your mother, and ½ of a kiss to Nellie, and ⅟200 of a kiss to Emsie, ⅟2000000 of a kiss to yourself. So with fondest love, I am, my darling,

"Your loving Uncle,
"C. L. Dodgson."

And at the end of this letter, teeming with fun and laughter, could anything be sweeter than this postscript?

"I've thought about that little prayer you asked me to write for Nellie and Emsie. But I would like first to have the words of the one I wrote for *you*, and the words of what they say *now*, if they say any. And then I will pray to our Heavenly Father to help me to write a prayer that will be really fit for them to use."

In letter-writing, and even in his story-telling, Lewis Carroll made frequent use of italics. His own speech was so emphatic that his writing would have looked odd without them, and many of his cleverest bits of nonsense would have been lost but for their aid.

Another time Isa ended a letter to him with "All join me in lufs and kisses." Now Miss Isa was away on a visit and had no one near to join her in such a message, but that is what she would have put had she been at home, and this is the letter he wrote in reply:

> "7 Lushington Road, Eastbourne,
> "Aug. 30, '90.

"Oh, you naughty, naughty, bad, wicked little girl! You forgot to put a stamp on your letter, and your poor old Uncle had to pay *Twopence*! His *last* Twopence! Think of that. I shall punish you severely for this, once I get you here. So tremble! Do you hear? Be good enough to tremble!

"I've only time for one question to-day. Who in the world are the 'all' that join you in 'lufs and kisses'? Weren't you fancying you were at home and sending messages (as people constantly do) from Nellie and Emsie, without their having given any? It isn't a good plan—that sending messages people haven't given. I don't mean it's in the least *untruthful*, because everybody knows how commonly they are sent without having been given; but it lessens the pleasure of receiving messages. My sisters write to me 'with best love from all.' I know it isn't true, so don't value it much. The other day the husband of one of my 'child-friends' (who always writes 'your loving') wrote to me and ended with 'Ethel joins me in kindest regards.' In my answer I said (of course in fun)—'I am not going to send Ethel kindest regards, so I won't send her any message *at all*.' Then she wrote to say she didn't even know he was writing. 'Of course I would have sent best love,' and she added that she had given her husband a piece of her mind. Poor Husband!

> "**Your always loving Uncle,**
> "**C.L.D.**"

These initials were always joined as a monogram and written backward, thus, ☙, which no doubt, after the years of practice he had, he dashed off with an easy flourish. His general writing was not very legible, but when he was writing for the press he was very careful. "Why should the printers have to work overtime because my letters are ill-formed and my words run into each other?" he once said, and Miss Bowman has put in her little volume the facsimile of a diary he once wrote for her, where every letter was carefully formed so that Isa could read every word herself.

"They were happy days," she writes, "those days in Oxford, spent with the most fascinating companion that a child could have. In our walks about the old town, in our visits to the Cathedral or Chapel Hall, in our visits to his friends, he was an ideal companion, but I think I was always happiest when we came back to his rooms and had tea alone; when the fire glow (it was always winter when I stayed in Oxford) threw fantastic shadows about the quaint room, and the thoughts of the prosiest people must have wandered a little into fairyland. The shifting firelight seemed almost to etherealize that kindly face, and as the wonderful stories fell from his lips, and his eyes lighted on me with the sweetest smile that ever a man wore, I was conscious of a love and reverence for Charles Dodgson that became nearly an adoration."

"He was very particular," she tells us, "about his tea, which he always made himself, and in order that it should draw properly he would walk about the room, swinging the teapot from side to side, for exactly ten minutes. The idea of the grave professor promenading his book-lined study and carefully waving a teapot to and fro may seem ridiculous, but all the minutiæ of life received an extreme attention at his hands."

The diary referred to, which he so carefully printed for Isa, covered several days' visit to Oxford in 1888, which oddly enough happened to be in midsummer, and being her first, was never forgotten. It was written in six "chapters" and jotted down faithfully the happenings of each day. What little girl could resist the feast of fun and frolic he had planned for those happy days!

First, he met her at Paddington station; then he took her to see a panorama of the Falls of Niagara, after which they had dinner with a Mrs. Dymes, and two of her children, Helen and Maud, went with them to Terry's Theater to see "Little Lord Fauntleroy" played by Vera Beringer, another little actress friend of Lewis Carroll.

After this they all took the Metropolitan railway; the little Dymes girls got off at their station, but Isa and the Aged Aged Man, as he called himself, went on to Oxford. There they saw everything to be seen, beginning with Christ Church, where the "A.A.M." lived, and here and there Lewis Carroll managed to throw bits of history into the funny little diary. They saw all the colleges, and Christ Church Meadow, and the barges which the Oxford crews used as boathouses, and took long walks, and went to St. Mary's Church on Sunday, and lots of other interesting things.

Every year she stayed a while with him at Eastbourne, where she tells us she was even happier if possible. Her day at Eastbourne began very early. Her room faced his, and after she was dressed in the morning she would steal into the little passage quiet as a mouse, and sit on the top stair, her eye on his closed door, watching for the signal of admission into his room; this was a newspaper pushed under his door. The moment she saw that, she was at liberty to rush in and fling herself upon him, after which excitement they went down to breakfast. Then he read a chapter from the Bible and made her tell it to him afterwards as a story of her own, beginning always with, "Once upon a time." After which there was a daily visit to the swimming-bath followed by one to the dentist—he always insisted on this, going himself quite as regularly.

After lunch, which with him consisted of a glass of sherry and a biscuit, while little Miss Isa ate a good substantial dinner, there was a game of backgammon, of which he was very fond, and then a long, long walk to the top of Beachy Head, which Isa hated. She says:

"Lewis Carroll believed very much in a great amount of exercise, and said one should always go to bed physically wearied with the exercise of the day. Accordingly, there was no way out of it, and every afternoon I had to walk to the top of Beachy Head. He was very good and kind. He would invent all sorts of new games to beguile the tedium of the way. One very curious and strange trait in his character was shown in these walks. I used to be very fond of flowers and animals also. A pretty dog or a hedge of honeysuckle was always a pleasant event upon our walk to me. And yet he himself cared for neither flowers nor animals. Tender and kind as he was, simple and unassuming in all his tastes, yet he did not like flowers.... He knew children so thoroughly and well, that it is all the stranger that he did not care for things that generally attract them so much.... When I was in raptures over a poppy or a dog-rose, he would try hard to be as interested as I was, but even to my childish eyes it was an effort, and he would always rather invent some new game for us to play at. Once, and once only, I remember him to have taken an interest in a flower, and that was because of the folklore that was attached to it, and not because of the beauty of the flower itself.

"... One day while we sat under a great tree, and the hum of the myriad insect life rivaled the murmur of the far-away waves, he took a foxglove from the heap that lay in my lap, and told me the story of how it came by its name; how in the old days, when all over England there were great forests, like the forest of Arden that Shakespeare loved, the pixies, the 'little folks,' used to wander at night in the glades, like Titania and Oberon and Puck, and because they took great pride in their dainty hands they made themselves gloves out of the flowers. So the particular flower that the 'little folks' used came to be called 'folks' gloves.' Then, because the country people were rough and clumsy in their talk, the name was shortened into 'foxgloves,' the name that everyone uses now."

This special walk always ended in the coastguard's house, where they partook of tea and rock cake, and here most of his prettiest stories were told. The most thrilling part occurred when "the children came to a deep dark wood," always described with a solemn dropping of the voice; by that Isa knew that the exciting part was coming, then she crept nearer to him, and he held her close while he finished the tale. Isa, as was quite natural, was a most dramatic little person, so she always knew what emotions would suit the occasion, and used them like the clever little actress that she was.

We find something very beautiful in this intimacy between the grave scholar and the light-hearted, innocent little girl, who used to love to watch him in some of those deep silences which neither cared to break. This small maid understood his every mood. A beautiful sunset, she tells us, touched him deeply. He would take off his hat and let the wind toss his hair, and look seaward with a very grave face. Once she saw tears in his eyes, and he gripped her hand very hard as they turned away.

Perhaps, what caught her childish fancy more than anything else, was his observance of Sunday. He always took Isa twice to church, and she went because she wanted to go; he did not believe in forcing children in such matters, but he made a point of slipping some interesting little book in his pocket, so in case she got tired, or the sermon was beyond her, she would have something pleasant to do instead of staring idly about the church or falling asleep, which was just as bad. Another peculiarity, she tells us, was his habit of keeping seated at the entrance of the choir. He contended that the rising of the congregation made the choir-boys conceited.

One could go on telling anecdotes of Lewis Carroll and this well-beloved child, but of a truth his own letters will show far better than any description how he regarded this "star" child of his. So far as her acting went, he never spared either praise or criticism where he thought it just. Here is a letter criticising her acting as the little *Duke of York*:

"Ch. Ch. Oxford. Ap. 4, '89.

"MY LORD DUKE:—The photographs your Grace did me the honor of sending arrived safely; and I can assure your Royal Highness that I am very glad to have them, and like them *very* much, particularly the large head of your late Royal Uncle's little, little son. I do not wonder that your excellent Uncle Richard should say 'off with his head' as a hint to the photographer to print it off. Would your Highness like me to go on calling you the Duke of York, or shall I say 'my own darling Isa'? Which do you like best?

"Now, I'm gong to find fault with my pet about her acting. What's the good of an old Uncle like me except to find fault?"

Then follows some excellent criticism on the proper emphasis of words, explained so that the smallest child could understand; he also notes some mispronounced words, and then he adds:

"One thing more. (What an impertinent uncle! Always finding fault!) You're not as *natural* when acting the Duke as you were when you acted Alice. You seemed to me not to forget *yourself* enough. It was not so much a real prince talking to his brother and uncle; it was Isa Bowman talking to people she didn't care much about, for an audience to listen to. I don't mean it was that all *through*, but *sometimes* you were *artificial*. Now, don't be jealous of Miss Hatton when I say she was *sweetly* natural. She looked and spoke like a real Prince of Wales. And she didn't seem to know there was any audience. If you ever get to be a *good* actress (as I hope you will) you must learn to forget 'Isa' altogether, and *be* the character you are playing. Try to think 'This is *really* the Prince of Wales. I'm his little brother and I'm *very* glad to meet him, and I love him *very* much, and this is *really* my uncle; he is very kind and lets me say saucy things to him,' and *do* forget that there's anybody else listening!

"My sweet pet, I *hope* you won't be offended with me for saying what I fancy might make your acting better.

"**Your loving old Uncle,**
"**Charles.**

"X for Nellie.

"X for Maggie.   "X for Isa."

"X for Emsie.

The crosses were unmistakably kisses. He was certainly a most affectionate "Uncle." He rarely signed his name "Charles." It was only on special occasions and to very "special" people.

Here is another letter written to Isa's sister Nellie, thanking her for a "tidy" she made him. (He called it an Antimacassar.) "The only ordinary thing about it," Isa tells us, "is the date." The letter reads backward. One has to begin at the very bottom and read up, instead of reading from the top downward:

"Nov. 1, 1891.

"C.L.D., Uncle loving your! Instead grandson his to it give to had you that so, years 80 or 70 for it forgot you that was it pity a what and; him of fond so were you wonder don't I and, gentleman old nice very a was he. For it made you that *him* been have *must* it see you so: *Grandfather* my was, *then* alive was that, 'Dodgson Uncle' only the, born was *I* before long was that see you then But. 'Dodgson Uncle for pretty thing some make I'll now,' it began you when yourself to said you that, me telling her without, knew I course of and: ago years many great a it made had you said she. Me told Isa what from was it? For meant was it who out made I how know you do! Lasted has it well how and Grandfather my for made had you Antimacassar pretty that me give to you of nice so was it, Nellie dear my."

He had often written a looking-glass letter which could only be read by holding it up to a mirror, but this sort of writing was a new departure.

In one of her letters Isa sent "sacks full of love and baskets full of kisses."

"How badly you *do* spell your words!" he answered her. "I *was* so puzzled about the 'sacks full of love and baskets full of kisses.' But at last I made out that, of course, you meant a 'sack full of *gloves* and a basket full of *kittens.*'" Then he composed a regular nonsense story on the subject. Isa and her sisters called it the "glove and kitten letter" and read it over and over with much delight, for it was full of quaint fancies, such as Lewis Carroll loved to shower upon the children.

When "Bootle's Baby" was put upon the stage, Maggie Bowman, though but a tiny child, played the part of *Mignon*, the little lost girl, who walked into the hearts of the soldiers, and especially one young fellow, to whom she clung most of all. Lewis Carroll, besides taking a personal interest in Maggie herself, was charmed with the play, which appealed to him strongly, so when little Maggie came to Oxford with the company she was treated like a queen. She stayed four days, during which time her "Uncle" took her to see everything worth looking at, and made a rhyming diary for her which he called—

MAGGIE'S VISIT TO OXFORD

When Maggie once to Oxford came
    On tour as "Bootle's Baby,"
She said: "I'll see this place of fame,
    However dull the day be!"

So with her friend she visited
    The sights that it was rich in,
And first of all she poked her head
    Inside the Christ Church Kitchen.

The cooks around that little child
    Stood waiting in a ring;
And every time that Maggie smiled,
    Those cooks began to sing—
Shouting the Battle-cry of Freedom!

            "Roast, boil, and bake,
            For Maggie's sake!
            Bring cutlets fine
            For *her* to dine;
            Meringues so sweet
            For *her* to eat—
            For Maggie may be
            Bootle's Baby."

There are a great many verses describing her walks and what
she saw, among other wonders "a lovely Pussy Cat."

            And everywhere that Maggie went
            That Cat was sure to go—
            Shouting the Battle-cry of Freedom!

            "Miaow! Miaow!
            Come make your bow!
            Take off your hats,
            Ye Pussy Cats!
            And purr and purr

To welcome her—
For Maggie may be
Bootle's Baby!"

So back to Christ Church-not too late
  For them to go and see
A Christ Church Undergraduate,
  Who gave them cakes and tea.

    . . . . . .

In Magdalen Park the deer are wild
  With joy that Maggie brings
Some bread, a friend had given the child,
  To feed the pretty things.

They flock round Maggie without fear,
  They breakfast and they lunch,
They dine, they sup, those happy deer—
  Still as they munch and munch,
Shouting the Battle-cry of Freedom!

    "Yes, deer are we,
    And dear is she.
    We love this child
    So sweet and mild:
    We all are fed
    With Maggie's bread—
    For Maggie may be
    Bootle's Baby!"

    . . . . . .

They met a Bishop on their way—
  A Bishop large as life—
With loving smile that seemed to say
  "Will Maggie be my wife?"

Maggie thought not, because you see
  She was so very young,

> And he was old as old could be—
>   So Maggie held her tongue.
>
> "My Lord, she's Bootle's Baby; we
>   Are going up and down,"
> Her friend explained, "that she may see
>   The sights of Oxford-town."
>
> "Now, say what kind of place it is!"
>   The Bishop gayly cried,
> "The best place in the Provinces!"
>   The little maid replied.
>
>   .   .   .   .   .   .
>
> Away next morning Maggie went
>   From Oxford-town; but yet
> The happy hours she there had spent
>   She could not soon forget.
>
>   .   .   .   .   .   .
>
>   "Oxford, good-bye!
>   She seemed to sigh,
>   You dear old City
>   With gardens pretty,
>   And lawns and flowers
>   And College towers,
>   And Tom's great Bell,
>   Farewell! farewell!
>   For Maggie may be
>   Bootle's Baby!"

Here is just a piece of a letter which shows that Lewis Carroll could tease when he liked. It is evident that Isa washed to buy the "Alice" book in French, to give to a friend, so she naïvely wrote to headquarters to ask the price. This is the reply:

"**Eastbourne.**

"MY OWN DARLING ISA,—The value of a copy of the French 'Alice' is £45: but, as you want the 'cheapest' kind, and as you are a great friend of mine, and as I am of a very noble, generous disposition, I have made up my mind to a great sacrifice, and have taken £3, 10s, 0d, off the price, so that you do not owe me more than £41, 10s, 0d, and this you can pay me, in gold or bank notes, as soon as you ever like. Oh, dear! I wonder why I write such nonsense! Can you explain to me, my pet, how it happens that when I take up my pen to write a letter to you, it won't write sense. Do you think the rule is that when the pen finds it has to write to a nonsensical, good-for-nothing child it sets to work to write a nonsensical, good-for-nothing letter? Well, now I'll tell you the real truth. As Miss Kitty Wilson is a dear friend of yours, of course she's a sort of a friend of mine. So I thought (in my vanity) 'perhaps she would like to have a copy "from the author" with her name written in it.' So I sent her one—but I hope she'll understand that I do it because she's your friend, for you see I had never heard of her before; so I wouldn't have any other reason."

When he published his last long story, "Sylvie and Bruno," the dedication was to her, an acrostic on her name; but as "Sylvie and Bruno" will be spoken of later on, perhaps it will be more interesting to give the dainty little verses where they belong. He sent his pet a specially bound copy of the new book, with the following letter:

"Christ Church, May 16, '90.

"Dearest Isa:—I had this bound for you when the book first came out, and it's been waiting here ever since Dec. 17, for I really didn't dare to send it across the Atlantic—the whales are *so* inconsiderate. They'd have been sure to want to borrow it to show to the little whales, quite forgetting that the salt water would be sure to spoil it.

"Also I've been waiting for you to get back to send Emsie the 'Nursery Alice.' I give it to the youngest in a family generally, but I've given one to Maggie as well, because she travels about so much, and I thought she would like to have one to take with her. I hope Nellie's eyes won't get *quite* green with jealousy at two (indeed three) of her sisters getting presents, and nothing for her! I've nothing but my love to send her to-day, but she shall have *something some* day.—Ever your loving

"UNCLE CHARLES."

The "Nursery Alice" he refers to was arranged by himself for children "from naught to five" as he quaintly puts it. It contained twenty beautiful colored drawings from the Tenniel illustrations, with a cover designed by E. Gertrude Thomson, of whose work he was very fond. The words were simplified for nursery readers.

In another letter to Isa he talks very seriously about "social position."

"Ladies," he writes, "have to be *much* more particular in observing the distinctions of what is called 'social position,' and the *lower* their own position is (in the scale of 'lady' ship) the more jealous they seem to be in guarding it.... Not long ago I was staying in a house with a young lady (about twenty years old I should think) with a title of her own, as she was an earl's daughter. I happened to sit next to her at dinner, and every time I spoke to her she looked at me more as if she was looking down on me from about a mile up in the air, and as if she was saying to herself, 'How *dare* you speak to *me*! Why you're not good enough to black my shoes!' It was so unpleasant that next day at luncheon I got as far from her as I could.

"Of course we are all *quite* equal in God's sight, but we *do* make a lot of distinctions (some of them quite unmeaning) among ourselves!"

However, he was not always so unfortunate among great people, the "truly great" that is. In Lord Salisbury's house he was always a welcome and honored guest, for in a letter to "his little girl" from Hatfield House he tells her of the Duchess of Albany and her two children.

"She is the widow of Prince Leopold (the Queen's youngest son), so her children are a Prince and a Princess; the girl is Alice, but I don't know the boy's Christian name; they call him 'Albany' because he is the Duke of Albany.

"Now that I have made friends with a real live little Princess, I don't intend ever to *speak* to children who haven't any titles. In fact, I'm so proud, and I hold my chin so high, that I shouldn't even *see* you if we met! No, darlings, you mustn't believe *that*. If I made friends with a *dozen* Princesses, I would love you better than all of them together, even if I had them all rolled up into a sort of child-roly-poly.

"Love to Nellie and Emsie.—Your loving Uncle,

"C.L.D.
    "XXXXXXX
        "[kisses]."

Nothing could give us a better glimpse of the wholesome nature of this quiet "don" of ours than these letters to a little child; a wholesome child like himself, whose every emotion was to him like the page of some fairy book, to be read and read again. Isa Bowman could not know, child as she was, *what* she was to this man, who with all his busy life, and all his gifts and talents, and all his many friendships, was so curiously lonely. But later, when she was grown, and wrote the little book of memories from which we have drawn so many sweet lessons, she doubtless realized, as she rolled back the years, what they had been to her—and what to Lewis Carroll.

Chapter XIV

A Trip with Sylvie and Bruno

Is all our life, then, but a dream,
Seen faintly in the golden gleam
Athwart Time's dark resistless stream?

Bowed to the earth with bitter woe,
Or laughing at some raree-show,
We flitter idly to and fro.

Man's little day in haste we spend,
And from its merry noontide send
No glance to meet the silent end.

This beautiful dedication to little Isa Bowman, on the front page of "Sylvie and Bruno," was much prized by her on account of the double acrostic cleverly woven in the lines. The first letter of each line read downward was one way she could see her name, and the first three letters in the first line of each verse was another, but naturally the light-hearted child missed the note of deep sadness underlying the tuneful words. Lewis Carroll had reached that milestone in a man's life, not when he pauses to look backward, but when his one desire is to press forward to the heights—to the goal. His thoughts were not so much colored by memories of earlier years as by anticipation, even dreams of what the future might hold. Therefore, in our trip with Sylvie and Bruno into the realms of dreamland, we must bear in mind in reading the story that the man is the dreamer, and not the children, nor does he see quite through their eyes in his views of men and things. Children, as a rule, live in the present; neither the past nor the future perplexes them, and "Mister Sir," as little Bruno called their friend, the Dreamer, looked on these fairy children, dainty Sylvie and graceful Bruno, as gleams of light in his shadowy way, little passing gleams, as elusive as they were brilliant.

The day of the irresponsible, bubbling nonsense is over; we catch flashes of it now and then, but the fun is forced, and however much of a dear *Sylvie* may be, and however much of a darling *Bruno* may be, they are not *quite* natural.

In a very long and very serious preface, wholly unlike his usual style, the author tells us something of the history of the book. As early as 1867 the idea of "Sylvie and Bruno" first came to him in the shape of a little fairy tale which he wrote for *Aunt Judy's Magazine*, but it was not until long after the publication of "Alice Through the Looking-Glass" that he determined to turn the adventures of these fairy children into something more than stray stories. The public, at least, the insatiable children, wanted something more from him, and as the second "Alice" had been so satisfactory, he decided to venture again into the dream-world; he would not hurry about it; he would take his time; he would pluck a flower here and there as the years passed, and press it for safe-keeping; he would create something poetic and beautiful in the way of children, culled from the best of all the children he ever knew. This work should be a gem, cut and polished until its luster eclipsed all other work of his.

And so from 1874 to 1889, a period of fifteen years, he jotted down quaint fancies and bits of dialogue which he thought would work well into the story. During this interval he passed from the prime of life into serious middle age, though there was so little change in his outward living and in his general appearance (he was always very boyish-looking) that even he himself failed to recognize the gulf of time between forty-two and fifty-seven.

In this interval he had become deeply interested in the study of logic and when he began to gather together the mass of material he had collected for his book, he found so much matter which stepped outside of childish realms that he decided to please both the "grown-ups" and the youngsters by weaving it all into a story, which he accordingly did, with the result that he pleased no one.

The children would not take the trouble to wade through the interwoven love story, while their elders, who from experience had expected something fresh and breezy from the pen of Lewis Carroll, who longed to get away from the world of facts and logic and deep discussions which buzzed about them, were even more sorely disappointed.

All flights of genius are short and quick. Had our author sat down when the idea of a long story first came to him, and written it off in his natural style, "Sylvie and Bruno" might have been another of the world's classics; but he put too much thought upon it, and the chapters show most plainly where the pen was laid down and where taken up again.

But for all that the book sold well, chiefly, indeed, because it was Lewis Carroll who wrote it; though its popularity died down in a short time. About six years ago, however (1904), the enterprising publishers brought forth a new edition of the book, leaving out all the grown-up part, and bringing the fairy children right before us in all their simple loveliness. The experiment, so far as the story went, was most successful, and to those who have not a previous acquaintance with "Sylvie and Bruno" this little volume would give much more pleasure than the big two-volume original.

One of Lewis Carroll's special objects in writing this story was a sort of tardy appreciation of the much-despised boy. In the character of *Bruno* he has given us a sweet little fellow, but we cannot get over the feeling that he is a girl in boy's clothes, his bits of mischief are all so dainty and alluring; but we would like to beat him with, say, a spray of goldenrod for such a fairy child, every time he says politely and priggishly "Mister Sir" to his invisible companion. What boy was *ever* guilty of using such a term! The street urchin would naturally say "Mister," but the well-bred home boy would say "Sir," so the combination sounds absurd.

Sylvie and *Bruno* were supposed to be the fairies that teach children to be good, and to do this they wandered pretty well over the earth in their fairy way. Somehow we miss the real children through all their dainty play and laughter, but the pictures of the two children, by Harry Furniss, are beautiful enough to make us really believe in fairies. There is a question Lewis Carroll asks quite gravely in his book—"What is the best time for seeing Fairies?" And he answers it in truly Lewis Carroll style:

"The first rule is, that it must be a *very* hot day—that we may consider as settled: and you must be a *little* sleepy—but not too sleepy to keep your eyes open, mind. Well, and you ought to feel a little what one may call 'fairyish' the Scotch call it 'eerie,' and perhaps that's a prettier word; if you don't know what it means, I'm afraid I can hardly explain it; you must wait till you meet a Fairy and then you'll know.

"And the last rule is, that the crickets should not be chirping. I can't stop to explain that; you must take it on trust for the present.

"So, if all these things happen together, you have a good chance of seeing a Fairy, or at least a much better chance than if they didn't."

Later on he tells us the rule about the crickets. "They always leave off chirping when a Fairy goes by, ... so whenever you're walking out and the crickets suddenly leave off chirping you may be sure that they see a Fairy."

Another dainty description is *Bruno's* singing to the accompaniment of tuneful harebells, and the song was a regular serenade:

> Rise, oh, rise! The daylight dies,
>   The owls are hooting, ting, ting, ting!
> Wake, oh, wake! Beside the lake
>   The elves are fluting, ting, ting, ting!
> Welcoming our Fairy King,
>   We sing, sing, sing.
>
> Hear, oh, hear! From far and near
>   The music stealing, ting, ting, ting!
> Fairy bells adorn the dells
>   Are merrily pealing, ting, ting, ting!

Welcoming our Fairy King,
  We ring, ring, ring.

See, oh, see! On every tree
  What lamps are shining, ting, ting, ting!
They are eyes of fiery flies
  To light our dining, ting, ting, ting!
Welcoming our Fairy King,
  They swing, swing, swing.

Haste, oh, haste, to take and taste
  The dainties waiting, ting, ting, ting!
Honey-dew is stored——

But here *Bruno's* song came to a sudden end and was never finished. Fairies have the oddest ways of doing things, but then *Sylvie* was coming through the long grass, that charming woodland child that little *Bruno* loved and teased.

The artist put all his skill into the drawing of this tiny maiden, skill assisted by Lewis Carroll's own ideas of what a fairy-girl should look like, and the fact that Mr. Furniss took *seven years* to illustrate this book to the author's satisfaction and his own, shows how very particular both were to get at the spirit of the story.

Indeed, the great trouble with the story is that it is all spirit; there is no *real* story to it, and this the keen scent of everyday children soon discovered.

But in one thing it excels: the verses are every bit as charming as either the Wonderland or Looking-Glass verses, with all the old-time delicious nonsense. Take, for instance—

THE GARDENER'S SONG

He thought he saw an Albatross
  That fluttered round the lamp;
He looked again, and found it was
  A Penny-Postage-Stamp.

"You'd best be getting home," he said:
  "The nights are very damp!"

He thought he saw an Argument
  That proved he was the Pope;
He looked again, and found it was
  A Bar-of-Mottled-Soap.
"A fact so dread," he faintly said,
  "Extinguishes all hope!"

He thought he saw a Banker's-Clerk
  Descending from the Bus;
He looked again, and found it was
  A Hippopotamus.
"If this should stay to dine," he said,
  "There won't be much for us!"

He thought he saw a Buffalo
  Upon the chimney-piece;
He looked again, and found it was
  His Sister's-Husband's-Niece.
"Unless you leave this house," he said,
  "I'll send for the police!"

He thought he saw a Coach-and-Four
  That stood beside his bed;
He looked again, and found it was
  A Bear without a head.
"Poor thing!" he said, "poor, silly thing!
  It's waiting to be fed!"

He thought he saw a Garden-Door
  That opened with a key;
He looked again, and found it was
  A Double-Rule-of-Three.
"And all its mystery," he said,
  "Is clear as day to me!"

> He thought he saw a Kangaroo
>   That worked a coffee-mill;
> He looked again, and found it was
>   A Vegetable-Pill.
> "Were I to swallow this," he said,
>   "I should be very ill!"
>
> He thought he saw a Rattlesnake
>   That questioned him in Greek;
> He looked again, and found it was
>   The Middle-of-Next-Week.
> "The one thing I regret," he said,
>   "Is that it cannot speak!"

The gardener was a very remarkable person, whose time was spent raking the beds and making up extra verses to this beautiful poem; the last one ran:

> He thought he saw an Elephant
>   That practiced on a fife;
> He looked again, and found it was
>   A letter from his wife.
> "At length I realize," he said,
>   "The bitterness of Life!"

"What a wild being it was who sung these wild words! A gardener he seemed to be, yet surely a mad one by the way he brandished his rake, madder by the way he broke ever and anon into a frantic jig, maddest of all by the shriek in which he brought out the last words of the stanza.

"It was so far a description of himself that he had the *feet* of an elephant, but the rest of him was skin and bone; and the wisps of loose straw that bristled all about him suggested that he had been originally stuffed with it, and that nearly all the stuffing had come out."

In "Sylvie and Bruno," probably to a greater extent than in all his other books, are some clever caricatures of well-known people. The two professors are certainly taken from life, probably from Oxford. One is called "The Professor" and one "The Other Professor." The *Baron*, the *Vice-Warden* and *my Lady* were all too real, and as for the fat *Prince Uggug*, well, any kind feeling Lewis Carroll may have had toward boys when he fashioned *Bruno* had entirely vanished when *Prince Uggug* came upon the scene. All the ugly, rough, ill-mannered, bad boys Lewis Carroll had ever heard of were rolled into this wretched, fat, pig of a prince; but the story of this prince proved fascinating to the *real* little royalties to whom he told it during one Christmas week at Lord Salisbury's. Most likely he selected this story with an object, in order to show how necessary it was that those of royal blood should behave like true princes and princesses if they would be truly loved. Our good "don" was fond of pointing a moral now and then. *Uggug*, with all his badness, somehow appeals to the human child, far more than *Bruno*, with his baby talk and his old-man wisdom and his odd little "fay" ways. *Sylvie* was much more natural. *Bruno*, however, was a sweet little songster; it needed no urging to set him to music, and he always sang quite plainly when he had real rhymes to tackle. One of his favorites was called:

THE BADGERS AND THE HERRINGS

> There be three Badgers on a mossy stone,
>   Beside a dark and covered way.
> Each dreams himself a monarch on his throne,
>   And so they stay and stay—
> Though their old Father languishes alone,
>   They stay, and stay, and stay.
>
> There be three Herrings loitering around,
>   Longing to share that mossy seat.
> Each Herring tries to sing what she has found
>   That makes life seem so sweet
> Thus, with a grating and uncertain sound,
>   They bleat, and bleat, and bleat.
>
> The Mother-Herring, on the salt sea-wave,
>   Sought vainly for her absent ones;

The Father-Badger, writhing in a cave,
    Shrieked out, "Return, my sons!
You shall have buns," he shrieked, "if you'll behave!
    Yea buns, and buns, and buns!"

"I fear," said she, "your sons have gone astray.
    My daughters left me while I slept."
"Yes'm," the Badger said, "it's as you say.
    They should be better kept."
Thus the poor parents talked the time away,
    And wept, and wept, and wept.

But the thoughtless young ones, who had wandered from home, are having a good time, a rollicking good time, for the *Herrings* sing:

Oh, dear, beyond our dearest dreams,
    Fairer than all that fairest seems!
To feast the rosy hours away,
    To revel in a roundelay!
        How blest would be
        A life so free—
Ipwergis pudding to consume
And drink the subtle Azzigoom!

And if in other days and hours,
    'Mid other fluffs and other flowers,
The choice were given me how to dine—
    "Name what thou wilt: it shall be thine!"
        Oh, then I see
        The life for me—
Ipwergis pudding to consume
And drink the subtle Azzigoom!

The Badgers did not care to talk to Fish;
    They did not dote on Herrings' songs;
They never had experienced the dish
    To which that name belongs.

> "And, oh, to pinch their tails" (this was their wish)
>   "With tongs, yea, tongs, and tongs!"
>
> "And are not these the Fish," the eldest sighed,
>   "Whose mother dwells beneath the foam?"
> "They are the Fish!" the second one replied,
>   "And they have left their home!"
> "Oh, wicked Fish," the youngest Badger cried,
>   "To roam, yea, roam, and roam!"
>
> Gently the Badgers trotted to the shore—
>   The sandy shore that fringed the bay.
> Each in his mouth a living Herring bore—
>   Those aged ones waxed gay.
> Clear rang their voices through the ocean's roar.
>   "Hooray, hooray, hooray!'"

Most of Lewis Carroll's best nonsense rhymes abounded with all sorts of queer animals. In earlier years he had made quite a study of natural history, so that he knew enough about the habits of the animals who figured in his verses to make humorous portraits of them. Yet we know, apart from the earth-worms and snails of "little boy" days, he never cared to cultivate their acquaintance except in a casual way. He was never unkind to them, and fought with all his might against vivisection (which in plain English means cutting up live animals for scientific purposes), as well as against the cruel pastime of English cross-country hunting, where one poor little fox is run to earth and torn in pieces by the savage hounds. Big hunting, where the object was a man-eating lion or some other animal which menaced human life, he heartily approved of, but wanton cruelty he could not abide. Yet the dog he might use every effort to save from the knife of science did not appeal to him as a pet; he preferred a nice, plump, rosy-cheeked, bright-eyed, ringleted little girl—if *she* liked dogs, why, very well, only none of them in *his* rooms, thank you!

These fairy children, *Sylvie* and *Bruno*, travel many leagues in the story, for good fairies must be able to go from place to place very quickly. We find them in Elfland, and Outland, and even Dogland.

A quaint episode in this book is the loss of Queen Titania's baby.

"We put it in a flower," Sylvie explained, with her eyes full of tears. "Only we can't remember *which*!" And there's a real fairy hunt for the missing baby, which must have been found somewhere, for fairies are never completely lost. All through this fairy tale move real people doing real things, acting real parts, coming often in contact with their good fairies, but parting always on the borderland, bearing with them but a memory of the beautiful children, and an echo of *Sylvie's* song as it dies away in the distance.

> Say, what is the spell, when her fledglings are cheeping,
>   That lures the bird home to her nest?
> Or wakes the tired mother, whose infant is weeping,
>   To cuddle and croon it to rest?
> What's the magic that charms the glad babe in her arms,
>   Till it cooes with the voice of the dove?
> 'Tis a secret, and so let us whisper it low—
>   And the name of the secret is Love!
>   For I think it is Love,
>   For I feel it is Love,
>   For I'm sure it is nothing but Love!
>
> Say, whence is the voice that, when anger is burning,
>   Bids the whirl of the tempest to cease?
> That stirs the vexed soul with an aching—a yearning
>   For the brotherly hand-grip of peace?
>
> Whence the music that fills all our being—that thrills
>   Around us, beneath, and above?
> 'Tis a secret; none knows how it comes, how it goes;
>   But the name of the secret is Love!
>   For I think it is Love,
>   For I feel it is Love,
>   For I'm sure it is nothing but Love!

Say, whose is the skill that paints valley and hill,
    Like a picture so fair to the sight?
That decks the green meadow with sunshine and shadow,
    Till the little lambs leap with delight?
'Tis a secret untold to hearts cruel and cold,
    Though 'tis sung by the angels above,
In notes that ring clear for the ears that can hear—
    And the name of the secret is Love!
        For I think it is Love,
        For I feel it is Love,
For I'm sure it is nothing but Love!

Chapter XV

Lewis Carroll–Man and Child

Love was indeed the keynote of Lewis Carroll's life. It was his rule, which governed everything he did, whether it was a lecture on mathematics or a "nonsense" story to a group of little girls. It was, above all, his religion, and meant much more to him than mere church forms, though the beautiful services at Oxford always impressed him deeply. Living as he did, apart from the stir and bustle of a great city, in a beautiful old town, full of historic associations, the heart and center of English learning, where men had time for high thoughts and high deeds, it is no wonder that his ideals should soar beyond the limits of an everyday world, and no one who watched the daily routine of this quiet, self-contained, precise "don" could imagine how the great heart beneath the student's clerical coat craved the love of those for whom he truly cared.

Outsiders saw only a busy scholar, absorbed in his work, to all appearances somewhat of a recluse. It is true, however, that his last busy years, devoted to a book on "Symbolic Logic," kept him tied to his study during most of the Oxford term, and that in consequence he had little time for sociability, if he wished to complete his work.

The first part of "Symbolic Logic" was published in 1896, and although sixty-four years old at the time, his writing and his reasoning were quite as clear as in the earlier days. He never reached the point of "going down hill." Everything that he undertook showed the vigorous strain in him, and though the end of his life was not far off, those who loved him were never tortured by a long and painful illness. As he said of himself, his life had been so singularly free from the cares and worries that assail most people, the current flowed so evenly that his mental and physical health endured till the last.

In later years the tall, slim figure, the clean-shaven, delicate, refined face, the quiet, courteous, rather distant manner, were much commented upon alike by friends and strangers. With "grown-ups" he had always the air of the absent-minded scholar, but no matter how occupied, the presence of a little girl broke down the crust of his reserve and he became immediately the sunny companion, the fascinating weaver of tales, the old, enticing Lewis Carroll.

But he was above all things what we would call "a settled old bachelor." He had little "ways" essentially his own, little peculiarities in which no doubt he took a secret and childish pride. With children these were always more or less amusing.

If he was going on a railway journey, for instance, he mapped out every minute of his time; then he would calculate the amount of money to be spent, and he always carried two purses, arranging methodically the sums for cabs, porters, newspapers, refreshments, and so forth, in different partitions, so he always had the correct change and always secured the best of service. In packing he was also very particular; everything in his trunk had to be separately wrapped up in a piece of paper, and his luggage (he probably traveled with several trunks) always preceded him by a day or so, while his only encumbrance was a well-known little black bag which he always carried himself.

In dress, he was also a trifle "odd." He was scrupulously neat and very scholarly in appearance, with frock coat and immaculate linen, but he never wore an overcoat no matter how cold the weather, and in all seasons he wore a pair of gray and black cotton gloves and a tall hat.

He had a horror of staring colors, especially in little girls' dresses. He loved pink and gray, but any child visiting him, who dared to bring with her a dress of startling hue, such as red or green or yellow, was forbidden to wear it in his company.

His appetite was unusually small, and he used to marvel at the good solid food his girl friends managed to consume. Once, when he took a special favorite out to dine, he warned his hostess to be careful in helping her as she ate far too much.

In writing, he seldom sat down; how he managed we are not told, but most likely his desk was a high one.

He was a great walker in all winds and weather. Sometimes he overdid it, and came home with blistered feet and aching joints, sometimes soaked to the skin when overtaken by an unexpected rain; but always elated over the distance he had traveled. He forgot, in the sheer delight of active exercise, that he was not absolutely proof against illness, and that added years needed added care; and as we find that the many severe colds which now constantly attacked him came usually in the winter, there is every reason to believe that human imprudence weakened a very strong constitution, and that Lewis Carroll minus an overcoat meant Lewis Carroll plus a very bad cold.

On one occasion (February, 1895) he was laid up with a ten days' attack of influenza, with very high and alarming fever. Yet as late as December, 1897, a few weeks before his death, he boasted of sitting in his large room with no fire, an open window, and a temperature of 54°.

Another time he had a severe attack of illness which prevented him from spending his usual Christmas with his sisters at Guildford. He was a prisoner in his room for over six weeks, but in writing to one of his beloved child friends he joked over it all, his only regret being the loss of the Christmas plum pudding.

From the time of the publication of "Alice in Wonderland" Lewis Carroll was a man of independent means; had he wished, he might have lived in great style and luxury, but being simple and unassuming in his tastes, he was content with his spacious book-lined rooms, with their air of solid, old-fashioned comfort. The things around him, which he cared for most, were things endeared by association, from the pictures of his girl friends upon the walls to that delightful and mysterious cupboard in which generations of children had loved to rummage.

He was fond, too, of practicing little economies where one would least expect them. In giving those enjoyable dinners of his, he kept neatly cut pieces of cardboard to slip under the plates and dishes; table mats he considered a needless luxury and a mere waste of money, while the cardboard could be renewed from time to time, with little trouble or expense. But if he wished to buy books for himself or take some little girl pet off for a treat, he never seemed to count the cost, and he gave so generously that many a child of the old days has cause to remember. On one occasion he found a crowd of ragamuffins surrounding the window of a shop where they were cooking cakes. Something in the wistful glances of the little street urchins stirred him strangely as he was passing by, a little girl on either side of him. Suddenly he darted into the shop, and before long came out, his arms piled with the freshly made cakes, which he passed around to the hungry, big-eyed little fellows, leaving the small girls inside the shop, where they could enjoy the pretty scene which stamped itself forever in their memories.

His charities were never known, save that he gave freely in many directions. He was opposed to *lending* money, but if the case was worthy he was willing to *give* whatever was necessary, and this he did with a kindliness and grace peculiarly his own. He was interested in hospitals, especially the children's wards, and many a donation of books and pictures and games and puzzles found their way to these pathetic little sufferers, whose heavy hours were lightened by his thoughtfulness. Hundreds of the "Alice" books were given in this fashion and many a generous check anonymously sent eased the pain of a great big sorrowful world of sick children. After his death his old friends, wishing that something special should be done to honor his memory, subscribed a sum of money to endow a cot in the Children's Hospital in Great Ormond Street. This was called the "Alice in Wonderland" cot, and is devoted to little patients connected with the stage, in which he had always shown such an interest.

Much has been said of Lewis Carroll's reverence for sacred things; from the days of his solemn little boyhood this was a most noticeable trait of his character. He had, as we have seen, no "cut and dried" notions regarding religion, but he was old-fashioned in many of his ideas, and while he did not believe in making the Sabbath a day of dull, monotonous ordeal, he set it apart from other days, and made of it a beautiful day of rest. He put from him the weekly cares and worries, brushing aside all work, and requiring others connected with him to do likewise. He wrote to Miss E. Gertrude Thomson, who was illustrating "The Three Sunsets"—his last collection of poems—(published in 1898), that she would oblige him greatly by making no drawings or photographs for him on a Sunday.

When he could, especially during the last years of his life, he gave a sermon, either at Guildford, Eastbourne, or at Oxford. It was through his influence that the Sunday dinner hour at the University was changed from seven to six o'clock, in order that the servants might be able to attend services. These he often conducted himself, and sometimes, in his direct and earnest talks, appealed to many who were hard to reach. Above all, however, a flock of children inspired his best efforts, and the simple fact that he always practiced what he preached made his words all the more impressive. In short, but for the impediment in his speech, he would have made a great preacher.

It was this simple, childlike faith of his that kept him always young—in touch with the youth about him. Old age was never associated with him, and constant exercise made him as lithe and active as a boy. There is an amusing tale of some distinguished personage who went to call on the Rev. Mr. Hatch, and while waiting for his host, he heard a great commotion under the dining table. Stooping down he saw children's legs waving frantically below, and, diving down himself to join the fun, he came face to face with Lewis Carroll, who had been the foundation of this animated, wriggling mass.

On another occasion Lewis Carroll went to call upon a friend, and finding her out, was about to turn away, when the maid, who had come from the front door to answer the bell at the gate, gave a startled cry—for the door had blown shut, and she was locked out of the house. Lewis Carroll was, as usual, equal to the occasion; he borrowed a ladder from some kind neighbor, climbed in at the drawing-room window, and after performing numerous acrobatic feats of the "small boy" type, managed to open the front door for the anxious maid.

His constant association with children made his activity in many ways equal to theirs. He certainly could outwalk them, for eighteen to twenty miles could not daunt him, and many a small girl who was brave enough to accompany him on what he called "a short walk" had tired feet and aching joints when the walk was over.

On December 23, 1897, he made ready for his yearly visit to Guildford, where he spent the usual happy Christmas, but in the early part of the New Year a slight hoarseness heralded the return of his old enemy—influenza. At first there seemed to be nothing alarming in his illness, but the disease spread very rapidly. The labored breathing, the short, painful gasps, quickly sapped his strength. On January 14, 1898, before his anxious family could quite realize it, the blow had fallen; the life which had meant so much to them, to everyone, went out, as Lewis Carroll folded his hands, closed his eyes, and said with that unquestioning faith, which had been his mainstay through the years: "Father, Thy will be done!"

Through the land there was mourning. Countless children bowed their sunny heads as the storm of grief passed over them, and it seemed as if, during the quiet funeral, a hush had come upon the world. They laid him to rest beneath the shadow of a tall pine, and a pure white cross bearing his own name and the name of "Lewis Carroll" rose to mark the spot, that the children who passed by might never forget their friend.

It seems, indeed, now that the years have passed, that the Angel of Death was very gentle with this fair soul. After all, does he not live in the happy fun and laughter he has left behind him, and will not the coming generations of children find in the wonder tales the same fascination that held the children of long ago? While childhood lasts on earth, while the memory of him lives in millions of childish hearts, Lewis Carroll can never die.

— THE END —

Made in the USA
Monee, IL
07 July 2026

56551325R00132